INTRODUCTION TO HERMENEUTICS

INTRODUCTION
TO
HERMENEUTICS

René Marlé, S.J.

HERDER AND HERDER

1967
HERDER AND HERDER NEW YORK
232 Madison Avenue, New York 10016

Original edition: *Le problème théologique de l'herméneutique,*
Paris, Editions de l'Orante, 1963.
Translated by E. Froment and R. Albrecht.

Nihil obstat: Leo J. Steady, Censor Librorum
Imprimatur: ✠Robert F. Joyce, Bishop of Burlington
May 16, 1967

Library of Congress Catalog Card Number: 66–13071
© 1967 by Herder and Herder, Inc.
Manufactured in the United States

Contents

INTRODUCTION TO HERMENEUTICS

Preface

NEXT TO that of the "historical Jesus,"[1] the most consistently discussed problem in Protestant theology in past years has been the problem of hermeneutics. As we shall see, hermeneutics has also been something of a problem in Catholic theology, though for different reasons and in different ways. The present work does not pretend to enumerate all the factors involved in the hermeneutical question, whether Catholic or Protestant; rather, its aim is only to make known the major contributions to hermeneutical theology, to point out the issues at the heart of the dispute (and these are not always easy to determine), and thus to provide an introduction to a field of research which has become so characteristic of the theology of our time.

The reader will perhaps not be surprised to find that most of our references are to German authors. While the problem of hermeneutics is not exclusively their domain, it is incontestable that among German theologians hermeneutics is most often taken up as a distinct speculative problem. For our own purposes, therefore, even though this specialization sometimes leads to narrowness, it also helps us to localize the major areas of thought; and even the occasional narrowness of the authors cited is an indication that we must strive to increase our awareness of the very important questions which hermeneutics raises.

R. M.

1. See James M. Robinson, *A New Quest of the Historical Jesus,* Naperville and London, 1959.

CHAPTER ONE

An Old Problem Is Resumed

THE THEOLOGICAL PROBLEM of hermeneutics, in the precise form
in which it appears today, is par excellence a modern problem.
Even though the major criticisms were already taking form in
the 18th and 19th centuries, it is only in the past few years, as
we shall see, that hermeneutics has come to be recognized as a
key theological issue.

Yet the "new" problem of hermeneutics has been proposed in
so many different ways that even those who insist upon its late
originality are led, as a result of the importance they rightly
accord it, to research its prehistory and study the past in order to
acquire a better perspective of present understanding of and insight into the hermeneutical problem. And in any case, it would
be naïve to think that preceding centuries entirely ignored in-
quiring into a matter which now so preoccupies our contemporaries.

By briefly recalling some of these earlier efforts in hermeneutical theology, and examining the implicit solutions contributed
then to the problem, we will thus be in a better position carefully to broaden our perspectives, and to benefit from past errors
and advances in defining more concisely our path of inquiry.
This is not to deny, of course—indeed, it is to affirm—that all

earlier attempts to solve the theological problem of hermeneutics are of no value today.

Hermeneutics as such is by no means a new problem. It can be generally defined as the science of the methods of the true interpretation of what is real, and this takes into special account research and reflection on the nature and principles of these methods. In its theological meaning, hermeneutics is the science of the methods of the true interpretation of Scripture. The word comes from the Greek *"hermeneuein,"* which means inclusively to express, to explain, to translate, and to interpret. Hermes was the divine messenger who announced, made known, and understood the thought of the gods. (He was also the god of cunning and trickery, and of theft; but that is not to our purpose.) To Hermes was attributed the invention of those things which serve to communicate, especially language and writing.

It was not, therefore, left to Christianity to invent the problem of hermeneutics, at least in its specifically theological context; it was already well known in Greek antiquity, when the hermeneutists were preoccupied with ascertaining the meaning of the myths that had been transmitted; and in general, the meaning of the poetical works, especially the Homeric writings. An entire division of culture, so to speak, was dedicated to the interpretation of these fundamental data, namely, the trilogy of grammar, rhetoric, and poetics. Aristotle in particular was concerned with establishing their laws. Along with the effort to master the pure techniques of language, moreover, which would allow for a true grasp of the literal meaning of a text, there also arose an effort at interpretation which sought to attain a more profound, interpretative understanding of the same text; this can be seen in the moralizing of the Stoics, and in the allegorizing of Alexandrian Hellenism.

This bifurcation of a text from its significance, of a tradition

from a sense that would render it meaningful, became the fundamental principle of the inevitable problem of hermeneutics—
inevitable, as we have shown, because it coincided with the rise
of critical understanding, of reason, of logos.

Although of a different genius, Judaism could not fail to encounter the problem of hermeneutics. The canon of Scripture,
and the divine Law contained in it, had to give meaning to and
rule the lives of the Israelites in a variety of ever new situations.
Hence the need arose for commentary, for authorized interpretation of the Law and Scripture. This was provided by the *mid-
rash,* which itself took two forms: the *halacha,* which explained
the Law with a dominant concern for juridical legalism; and
the *haggadah,* which offered interpretation in a less restricted
way through edifying stories and thoughts. In both cases, however, the concern was to explain and continue a tradition which
was in evidence in preserved documents, but which was in need
of further clarification in order for it to enlighten, and in fact
govern, the lives of men and the community.

It is true that Jesus was anything but a rabbinical commentator
on the Law, and that he did not deal directly with "problems"
in his teaching; but even so, he did not hesitate to give a completely new solution to the fundamental question of the meaning
of those Scriptures which informed the whole life of the people
of Israel. The Gospel, in fact, says that "he interpreted to them
in all the Scriptures the things concerning himself" (Lk. 24, 27).
He came to fulfill the Law (Mt. 5, 17), to restate it (Mt. 5, 21–28),
to establish a new covenant with man, thus showing all at once
the meaning of the Law, of the Jewish traditions, and of his own
mission. The New Testament itself is the resumption of a new
interpretation of the Scriptures, a new law.

The originality of this interpretation of the Law and the Scriptures did not result from some new intellectual advance in learn-

ing, but from a fact, an event: the coming and the fulfillment of the kingdom of God in the person, in the life, death, and resurrection of Jesus Christ. However, its originality is not absolute. In his *Old Testament Theology*,[1] Gerhard von Rad has shown how Israel, in the light of new divine interventions, continued to reinterpret its past and the Scriptures which contained it. However, because of its total and definitive character, this intervention of God in the person of Jesus had to introduce history, in a decisive way, to the principles of interpretation of the salvific Word. With the coming of the Messiah, the passage was made from figure, from image, to reality.

Thus a new principle of hermeneutics was introduced by the Christ event. The distinction was no longer made between a text and its true meaning; rather, a relationship was introduced between the meaning of a text and the historical situation of him who brought this meaning to light and who appropriated it. The problem of hermeneutics—regardless of the way in which it was first recognized and named—has ever since been presented as anything but a speculative problem. Essentially and above all, it became and has continued to be an existential problem.

However, that does not mean that difficult speculative questions of a hermeneutical nature do not arise. It was characteristic of the Scriptures which nourished the faith of Israel that they were ever "old" and ever "new." In a like manner, regarding the question of the original nature of the witness to Jesus Christ in what came to be called the New Testament, does one say that it is essentially a continuation of the Old Testament, or is it essentially something which is radically new? And what is the precise connection between these two expressions of the same word of God?

These matters, it is well known, have occupied theologians

1. New York, 1962.

throughout the entire history of the Church. In a synthetic way, they have been taken up once again by modern hermeneutical theology. We say "synthetic" and "once again" because the principal difference between former and modern hermeneutical theology is that the latter has achieved, through a synthetic comprehension of the various aspects of this old problem, a more thoughtful grasp of all that is involved; and has not ignored or necessarily depreciated the often astonishing efforts and the occasionally inspired successes of past centuries.

Moreover, if a more thorough study of the problem of hermeneutics has led, especially since the Christ event, to a recognition of the important connection between history and the meaning of a text to be interpreted, then that is all the more reason why research into the history of hermeneutics is an essential prerequisite of hermeneutical science. Indeed, under the article "Hermeneutik" in the third edition of the encyclopedia *Die Religion in Geschichte und Gegenwart,* Gerhard Ebeling, one of the most representative theologians in present hermeneutical research (as we shall see), declares that "the nature of hermeneutics necessarily implies a backward look into its own history."[2]

* * *

During one entire period of the history of the Church, the problem of hermeneutics was experienced, rather than thematically posed. The typological interpreting of the Letter to the Hebrews, the more directly allegorizing interpreting of the Letter to Barnabas, the moralizing tone of the First Letter of St. Clement of Rome, are all examples of practical solutions of the problem. Gnosticism and Marcionism, with their rejection or depreciation of parts of Scripture, gave rise to hermeneutical

2. Tübingen, 1959.

solution by way of necessary consequence: faced with these dangerous trends, and with the interpretation that Judaism continued to give the Old Testament, the Church had to formulate the true meaning of Scripture, and, in general, the true meaning of everything through which divine revelation was expressed.

During this same period the Church was also faced with the pressing problem of the "rule of faith," and solved it, while refuting the contentions of Marcionism and Gnosticism, by fixing the canon of Scripture and affirming the apostolic authority.

In the Christian world itself—that is, apart from direct and necessary theological confrontation with heretical teachings—the first great consideration of the problem of hermeneutics can be attributed to Origen. Moreover, the work in which he takes up this problem, in his *Hexapla,* appears to be inextricably exegetical and systematic, but in such a way that this becomes the very heart of the matter. Henri de Lubac, in fact, did not even think it necessary to choose another point of view than Origen's when he set forth the teachings of the great Alexandrian. If the title of de Lubac's work, *Histoire et Esprit,* expresses the scope of his own perspectives, and at the same time their "modernness," the subtitle significantly tells its direct objective: *L'intelligence des Ecritures d'après Origène.*[3]

Origen's edition of the *Hexapla* is sufficient evidence that he strove with great care to establish and rigorously study the text of Scripture. However, the extent of his efforts to find the definitive meaning of these texts—that is, in this case, the "spiritual" meaning—is equally well known. But because it is outside the framework of our study to analyze the exact nature of this "spiritual sense" which Origen attempted to determine, the various ways in which it is determined, and its connection

3. Paris, 1950.

with the literal and the historical sense, we will refer only to the more important works dedicated to this matter. It must also suffice to note that it is not by chance that even today Origen retains the attention of so many scholars who are sensitive to the more actual and vital questions of theology.[4]

It would be false to think that Origen, because of the basic attention he gave to the problem of hermeneutics, was some kind of exception in the theology of early Christianity, for in fact the theology of that time was dominated to a large extent by the rivalry between the schools of Alexandria and Antioch. As Jacques Guillet has shown,[5] there was never much opportunity either to simplify or to solidify the opposition between these two schools, since it stemmed from two different conceptions of what hermeneutics was: the Alexandrian school (the Catechetical school) striving to find the deeper "spiritual" sense of a text, the Antiochene being concerned with finding its true literal meaning. Here again, contemporary historians and theologians have come to recognize that what was actually at stake in these controversies, what appeared to be a question of method, was really a matter of the understanding of the faith.

It was not in the East alone that theological problems were in embryo largely hermeneutical problems. We can discern in Western theology similar tensions as those between the schools of Alexandria and Antioch: St. Jerome was a proponent of the literal school, while St. Ambrose and St. Hilary were representatives of the spiritual school. The similarity can be made even more precise between East and West, for St. Augustine, like Origen, united in himself the two preoccupations, and thus

4. See, for example, Jean Daniélou, *Origen,* New York, 1955. See also "The Recent Revival of Origen Studies," in *Theological Studies* 24, 1963, p. 250.

5. "Les exégèses d'Alexandrie et d'Antioche, conflit ou malentendu?", in *Recherches de science religieuse* 34, 1947, pp. 257–302.

established the foundations for an especially fruitful hermeneutics. As orator and grammarian he always remained the literalist, he minutely scrutinized the words of Scripture; but as the Neoplatonist philosopher, as the allegorist—under the influence of St. Ambrose—he was liberated from this close textual literalism, so much so that the principle of his hermeneutics is related to the whole of his theory of *signum* and *res,* which is at the heart of his theological reflection.

De Lubac has also shown that even at the time of medieval exegesis, the critical problem still was that of hermeneutics, though all its implications had not yet been fully disengaged.[6] In any case, research on the meaning of Scripture seems to have been the way of questing for the true meaning and essential content of the Christian faith during the Middle Ages. In the Introduction to the first volume of *Exégèse médiévale,* however, de Lubac points out that the authors he is discussing are "most often not exegetes in the modern and specialized meaning of the word," and that the examination of their thought which he is attempting is "not so much a contribution to the history of exegesis, properly speaking, as to the history of theology, or rather of Christian thought and spirituality in general."[7] Ancient Christian exegesis, he explains further on, is a "complete act." "The more it is studied," he continues, "the more one realizes the breadth of the field, the complexity of its implications, the depths of its substructures, and the originality of its construction. With varying nuances it brings out once again the amazing newness of the Christ event. It sets in motion a dialectic, often subtle, of the before and the after; it defines the connections between historical and spiritual reality, between

6. *Exégèse médiévale. Les quatre sens de l'Ecriture,* Paris, 1959 (vols. I and II) and 1961 (vol. III).
7. Vol. I, p. 11.

society and the individual, between time and eternity; it contains, as we would say today, an entire theology of history, one closely related to a theology of Scripture. . . . In short, ancient Christian exegesis was something more than just an ancient form of exegesis. It was 'the weave' of Christian art and literature; it was, in one of its essential aspects, ancient Christian thought. It was the principal form which for quite a long time clothed the Christian synthesis. In any case, it was the instrument which allowed for the construction of such a synthesis, and it is today one of the angles from which this synthesis can be most advantageously approached."[8]

We can see, therefore, that the relation between modern and earlier theological thought is much greater than we would ordinarily think. We can also recognize the very substantial importance of several earlier works which would perhaps in some quarters be written off as merely pragmatic or irrelevant, but which are actually quite valuable for the perspective they give to contemporary hermeneutical investigation.

From the 13th century on, the problem of hermeneutics began to take a different turn, and was no longer considered the central theological issue. It would be gratuitous were we to explain the prevalence of philosophical speculation within theology at that time.

During the time of the Reformation, however, hermeneutics returned to the forefront, and with great urgency, not only because it would assist in supporting the new Reformed theses professedly based on Scripture, point by point and detail by detail; not only because it was the inevitable development of the cult of the Bible which the Reformation had resolved to advance; but mainly because of the principle "*sola Scriptura*," which the Reformation claimed as its only and entire basis.

8. *Ibid.,* pp. 16–17.

And indeed, *sola Scriptura* was actually the introduction into Christianity of a new hermeneutical principle; and this introduction brought about not only a new understanding of faith, but also a new Christian faith, a new Church.

The principle *sola Scriptura* did not merely demand the rejection of every rule of faith and an interpretation outside of Scripture; it also implied that Scripture itself could render its own meaning of itself. Scripture was "*per sese certissima, facillima, apertissima, sui ipsius interpres, omnium probans, judicans et illuminans.*" Luther knew, of course, that there were obscure passages in Scripture, but he was convinced that the essential reality, at least, was clear. This living word of salvation, this *viva vox Evangelii,* could not fail to be heard by every loyal soul who approached Scripture in faith. Thus, of its own accord, *sola Scriptura* developed into a second principle of hermeneutics, according to which the whole of Scripture, or more precisely its very heart—*Christus trebit,* that which "produces" Christ—gives each passage its meaning. Luther took up this principle in his famous discussion of the conflict between *Gesetz* and *Evangelium* (Law and Gospel) (which remains one of the most frequently treated themes in Protestant theology, and which is a principle of hermeneutics). The application of this principle should actually have brought about a solution to the problem of the relation of the two testaments to one another; or to put it another way, to the problem of the meaning of the new reality introduced by Jesus Christ. It did not, however, but instead furnished, especially for the Lutherans, a way for Protestants to express and develop their understanding of the very object of the Christian faith.

It was only natural, then, faced with the Reformation, that the Council of Trent felt from its outset the need to formulate a principle of hermeneutics. It specified that the true meaning of Scripture could not be ascertained apart from the Church and tradition, which are in some way the place of its preservation and disclosure: ". . . to keep undisciplined minds under proper control, the Council decrees that no one should dare to rely on his own judgment in matters of faith and morals affecting the structure of Christian doctrine and to distort Sacred Scripture to fit meanings of his own that are contrary to the meaning that holy Mother Church has held and now holds; for it is her office to judge about the true sense and interpretation of Sacred Scripture. Nor should anyone dare to interpret Sacred Scripture contrary to the unanimous agreement of the Fathers, even though such interpretations are never going to be published."[9]

But Protestantism soon developed a kind of "orthodoxy" of its own, similar to that of Catholicism—one based, for example, on the principle of verbal inspiration, or on various theses which were taken from the confessions of faith and the works of the first Reformers. This introduction of a rule of faith which, regardless of its adherents' possible objections to the contrary, would be partly non-scriptural, has led not a few modern Protestant theologians to denounce it as a betrayal of the true principle of hermeneutics implied in *sola Scriptura;* and at the same time, as a perversion of the fundamental insight of Protestantism.

According to these theologians, the development of the historical-critical method at the beginning of modern times has allowed for the progressive recovery and improvement of the hermeneutical principle of the Reformation. In applying this method, today's exegete wants no other law than a continually

9. *La Foi catholique. Textes doctrinaux du Magistère de l'Eglise,* translated and presented by Gervais Dumeige, Paris, 1961. See Denzinger, no. 786.

confirmed fidelity to the true meaning of the text of Scripture; and for this reason he does not hesitate to subject the text to radical critique.

There is no denying the fact that the development and the even more demanding application of the historical-critical method was to bring about a relatively new relation of modern man to Scripture. Even if he is a believer, man of today no longer approaches the Bible in the same way that the Fathers of the ancient Church or theologians of the Middle Ages were able to. The questions he raises are no longer exclusively those which flow immediately from the faith. The basic harmony which once existed between the doctrine of faith, as it is found in the Bible, and the whole of culture, no longer exists. Rather, modern man conducts his investigation from a universe constructed outside the very realities of the faith.

In this context a new dimension, or at least a new aspect, of the problem of hermeneutics takes form. Previously, work on the meaning of a text was somewhat predetermined by the nature of the text, which was of itself of unquestionable validity. It had a fundamental relation to the reality it concerned; and it was only on the basis of this fundamental relation that relatively secondary differences of method or attitude could become operative. Formerly, the "problem of hermeneutics," considered in itself, was not spoken of; it was rather occupied with the *ars interpretandi,* with the *sensus Scripturae,* with the *regulae interpretationis,* or simply, exegesis. It was only in 1654 on the Protestant side, and in 1776 on the Catholic side, that the word "hermeneutics" appeared for the first time in the title of a theological work.

However, the radical transformation of outlook on the problem of hermeneutics was brought about mainly by the *Aufklärung,* and by the accompanying deliberate rejection of the distinction between sacred and profane hermeneutics, which until then had seemed obviable. The new spirit did not want to recognize any such hierarchy which might have preëxisted its investigation and which might, *a priori,* have limited its examination. If such a hierarchy were discovered, it was thought, it should happen within the research process itself; for it is this very process which the word "hermeneutics" attempts to translate, and which hermeneutical science attempts to analyze.

It was only natural, therefore, that philosophical speculation about the role of hermeneutics led to even further departure from its original theological definition. Thus for Friedrich Schleiermacher (1768–1834), hermeneutics was "the doctrine of the art of understanding," which, "starting from the simple fact of understanding, and dwelling on the nature of language and the relation between the one who speaks and the one who understands, develops its rules in a coherent system."[10] Wilhelm Dilthey (1833–1911) saw in it the basis for the humanities in general, that is to say, he saw hermeneutics as the very endeavor of philosophy. More recently, Martin Heidegger, in *Being and Time,* has designated the phenomenology of *Dasein* as hermeneutics.[11]

The attention which philosophers and theologians have given to the problem of hermeneutics is due to the conviction they seem to share about the relation, if not identity or connecting bond, between every object of human understanding and the

10. Cited by Ebeling in his article "Hermeneutik," in *Die Religion in Geschichte und Gegenwart,* col. 244.

11. "The phenomenology of *Dasein* is a hermeneutics in the original sense of the word, according to which it designates the word of interpretation . . . Insofar as it ontologically analyzes the historicity of *Dasein* as the condition for an ontic possibility of history, there is rooted in this hermeneutics what may be called 'hermeneutics' in a purely derivative manner, that is, the method of the historical sciences of the spirit." New York, 1962, pp. 37–38.

way objects are perceived. Here, however, we will confine our-self to discussing only the hermeneutical endeavors of theologians, and among them only those whose work is the more characteristic. As we shall see, though their individual delineations of the problem and their proffered solutions are quite independent, nevertheless the theologians themselves do share a definite intellectual climate, and definite singular objectives. This, now that we have concluded our brief historical survey, we shall attempt to describe.

CHAPTER TWO

The Origins of the Problem

IF IT IS TRUE, and it is, that the modern problem of hermeneutics could only have been introduced by the singular development of the historical-critical method during the last two centuries, it is nevertheless also true that its complexity and depth were barely understood by those who were first concerned with putting it to work. Quite on the contrary: the problem seemed to them a simple matter. It consisted merely in applying the scientific and critical method with ever greater exactness, a formula which had proved so fruitful in every other field of knowledge. It did not occur to them that the principle of hermeneutics could be different from the principles of science itself.

This possibility became apparent only when the importance of the historical-critical method itself was called into question, when its limits and thus its value were first realized. Martin Kähler (1835–1912) was the first Protestant theologian who critically and vigorously examined the mechanics of the historical-critical method, and its pretension of conveying the ultimate meaning of a text to which it was applied. In 1892, Kähler claimed that critical historians who thought that through science

they would be able to encounter the real, living Christ of the
Bible, were under an illusion. On the contrary, he said, "the
historical Jesus of modern writers conceals from us the living
Christ" of Scripture.[1] It is only lately, however, that the depth of
Kähler's insight has been rediscovered. Until now, his dissent
was for too long the only one, and his remarks made no noticeable impression.

KARL BARTH:
PROPHETICAL HERMENEUTICS

It was Karl Barth who rid critical science, as applied to the Bible,
of the unchallenged confidence it possessed, and who began the
debates, which still last, over the right way to examine and
express the scriptural text. The Preface to his *The Epistle to
the Romans*[2] can be considered the true beginning of contemporary thought regarding hermeneutics. Wrote Ebeling: "Barth's
The Epistle to the Romans is explicitly involved in the problem
of hermeneutics: the historical-critical method is not in itself
rejected, but relegated to become a simple preparation of the
task of understanding."[3]

What, then, were the principal ideas developed by Barth in
this Preface where, in answer to a number of critics who had
directed their remarks to him after publication of his first edition
of *Romans,* he detailed his project? Barth wrote that, while
undertaking a work rather free in style and deliberately theo-

1. *Der sogenannte historische Jesus und der geschichtliche, biblische
Christus,* Munich, 1953, p. 16.
2. New York, 1921.
3. See his article "Hermeneutik," in *Die Religion in Geschichte und
Gegenwart,* col. 256.

logical in scope, and regardless of any immediate objections, he had no intention of discounting the contributions made by the historical criticism which had been so fervently cultivated by previous generations. He reproached the exegetes and commentators before him for not having used the historical-critical method profitably, for being tied down by it while at the same time pretending to give a true "explanation" of the texts. For Barth, there was no such thing as a real "explanation."

The efforts of the historical-critical method, Barth continued, were only, or at least they should only attempt to be, a first effort at establishing the bare facts to be interpreted. Moreover, to the extent that they are not confined only to deciphering manuscripts and establishing a certain number of textual connections or concordances, any works which treat of the historical-critical method could well produce anything except definitive and unquestionable results—as their authors admit. The very diversity of their conclusions sufficiently proves this precariousness.

However, it was not the hypothetical character of such constructions which Barth found fault with, so much as the idea that they might be able, *even if only in principle,* to provide the ultimate meaning of the documents. "As long as there is only a question of establishing the bare facts to be interpreted [*was da steht*]," Barth said, "I have never dared, even in my dreams, to do anything other than sit attentively at the feet of such scholars as Jülicher or Lietzmann. I am again and again surprised at the modesty of their pretensions when I examine their attempts at true *understanding* and *interpretation.* By true understanding and interpretation I mean the creative drive which Luther exercised with such certain insight in his *Commentaries,* or which is characteristic of the systematic approach of Calvin. . . . How energetically did the latter, having first established the text [*was da steht*], then rethink the entire content and explain it, until the wall which separated the 1st century from the 16th became *transparent,* until St. Paul *speaks* and the man of the 16th century hears, until the dialogue between the original document and the reader comes to settle on the *subject matter,* so that there is no longer any distinction between then and now."

Modern authors tend to reproach the Reformers, Barth said, because they think their works are out of date, or for being slaves to the doctrine of inspiration. However, Barth asked, are not these same modern authors victims of the rather trite categories which they use to interpret the texts in question: such categories as emotions, experience, conscience, conviction? They are overly ingenious when they cast aside the "Pauline vessel" and think that they are discovering the true meaning of the text by merely calling upon the "personality" of the author, upon his "Damascus experience"—as if that could explain the most incredible of things—or upon later Judaism, Hellenism, or any other of the "demigods."

He continued: "I think that our basic efforts in regard to the text should give us no more than a paraphrase and should be the starting point which will lead to true interpretation of the text. In my opinion, critical historians may profit by being a little more critical." Barth explained that "more critical" meant more than just evaluating words and phrases in a given text. "*Krinein* applied to the historical texts means for me the measuring of all the words and phrases therein according to the criterion of that which the texts themselves are saying, unless, of course, a text is meaningless. Where there are answers, they must be related to the questions which they presuppose; and not with some other questions; and these presupposed questions must be related to the one cardinal question which embraces them all. The contents of the text must be made manifest only in the light of what can be said, and thus only in the light of what is really said."

Barth's fundamental idea was that St. Paul spoke of something which was really beyond his ability to express, and which alone can concern us—but which at the same time is not within our ability to understand. That "something" is, according to Barth, that God is God, and that his relation to man is Jesus Christ. This is St. Paul's "system," if one wants him to have one, his "presupposed dogmatics," his "Alexandrianism." What Barth wanted to understand is what St. Paul wanted to say. He was convinced that St. Paul had no desire to relate or even to express his own ideas or outlook, but only wanted to transmit a reality which imposed itself on him and determined his language. That reality was the revelation of God in Jesus Christ.

Barth was to take up this argument again in several passages of his *Church Dogmatics*,[4] especially in the second half of the first part. There he eloquently developed the Reformation principle of *Scriptura Scripturae interpres,* and explained how this principle of biblical hermeneutics had to inspire all hermeneutics in general. This principle, in fact, according to Barth, maintains the absolute importance of what is said in the text, and furthermore maintains that what is said must be understood in relation to the hermeneutical question and "reply." This fundamental conviction is the basis for all true hermeneutics. However, this submission to the object does not mean that the inquirer into the meaning of the text must lay aside his own thoughts, his own questions, his own ideas; that would mean giving up any attempt to understand what the text itself wishes to convey to him.

4. Naperville and London, 12 volumes in preparation. For an overview of Barth's theology, see Jerome Hamer, *Karl Barth,* Westminster, 1962, and on his theology of justification, see Hans Küng, *Justification,* New York, 1964.

Moreover, this procedure, besides being unfeasible, would not actually be submission but arrogance, for the requisite posture of submission need not mean that we "replace our thoughts and convictions with those of the prophets and the apostles; in other words, that instead of our own language, we speak the language of Canaan. Even if we learn the language of Canaan, we still remain influenced by its style, and we would not necessarily obtain the internal meaning of the message."

Barth is not a fundamentalist. He is only intent on safeguarding the absolute priority of the word of God over the act of the human spirit which understands it, and the absolute priority of the reality which is expressed by the texts over the understanding one gains of it by trying to assimilate it.

Dominated by this insight, Barth's theology is decidedly theocentric. One must recognize, moreover, that his work is characterized by strong prophetical undertones. It was always his concern to make things perfectly clear, and to this end he made use of all the resources of language and culture. His overriding concern, however, was always to convey the inexhaustible reality of divine revelation. In his Preface to *The Epistle to the Romans,* Barth remarked on the quandary, the distress of pastors who, at the beginning of their preaching office, had not gone beyond a mere "respect for history." This had been his own situation, he admitted, and it was this that prompted him to look for another way to approach the witness of the word of God. He was not, he insisted, a "spiritualist" (that is, in the pejorative sense of a visionary), as he had been accused of being. Nor was he a "professed enemy of critical theology." The theology he advocated was explicitly "critical." But he felt that historical criticism ought not to be accorded ultimate importance. Beyond historical criticism—and judging it—there is another: that critical scrutiny of our parochial categories and methods by the word of revelation to which the Scriptures attest. Criticism is, then, a first "property" of the word of God.

This basic attitude certainly entailed for Barth a large measure of freedom in dealing with the many details into which scientific analyses can all too easily dissolve. It was also, by the way, one of the reasons for Barth's humor, —and humor is seldom found in those who worship science as though it were divine. Finally, it was also doubtless the reason why Barth was not affected by those criticisms which were leveled at him on a logical and rational plane. He would quickly concede any number of points in this area if he thought it worth while. He did not hesitate continually to correct himself, because his purpose was not to furnish an airtight system with which the critic could find no fault. He knew that his chief concern was to bear witness to the living word which had in some way taken hold of him and which in spite of all brings to light these defects and short-comings.

What did affect Barth, however, was to see men who had become unable to hear or to convey the inexhaustible fullness of the divine word of revelation, who demeaned its wealth in the name of alleged criteria of intelligibility and in the name of a hermeneutics which—instead of being directed by its object, and finding in it its true capacity for understanding, as well as its liberty—limits its receptivity from the outset, and which, con-vinced that it functions in a necessary autonomy, in effect defers to tyrannical and destructive idols.

Barth hardly wasted his time in refuting such inadequate systems in order to justify his own in detail. Had he allowed his work as theologian to center on questions of method instead of on his proper object—which he allowed in a sense to reveal itself—he would have in part denied himself. Yet he did find it necessary to detail his point of view in opposition to that of

Rudolf Bultmann, especially in his *Rudolf Bultmann: An Attempt to Understand Him,* which we will refer to later, and also in several important passages of his *Church Dogmatics.*[5] And, in fact, Barth could not possibly have underestimated the singular influence exercised by his Marbourg colleague, nor forgotten the kinship of their first insights and their first projects.

Barth and Bultmann belonged to the same generation, were affected by the same influences, and made their own influence felt each in an original way, in opposition to their predecessors. They had undertaken the same work and shared the same hopes, but eventually they began to go further and further into opposite directions. Their opposition over the problem of hermeneutics, which involves all the others, is the opposition of two different temperaments, and two different spiritual and theological attitudes.

RUDOLF BULTMANN:
CRITICAL REQUIREMENTS AND THE
ENCOUNTER WITH HISTORY

The modern problem of hermeneutics can be seen taking on definite shape in the work of Bultmann, notably in his dissatisfaction with Barth's original position as outlined in *The Epistle to the Romans.* In the long review of this work in a 1922 edition of *Theologische Blätter,* Bultmann was unsparing in his praise, and professed his admiration of the work in more than one regard. However, he clearly outlined his disagreements with Barth over a number of important points.

The conception of faith developed by Barth seemed to Bult-

5. In his Preface to volume IV, Barth claims that he revised that volume as a result of his continuing dialogue with Rudolf Bultmann, even if he did not always mention him by name.

mann in some ways untenable, and above all exegetically unjustified. "That we may only believe that we do believe,"
Bultmann wrote, "is in no way the thought of St. Paul."

However, it was the method employed by Barth, as well as the
content of his interpretation, which Bultmann took issue with.
He sided with Barth against those who maintain a purely
"objective," "scientific," and "disinterested" exegesis, and also
agreed with him that "a text can be explained only if there is an
interior relation between it and the reality which it treats." It
is always necessary to approach the text on its own terms.
However, Bultmann said, Barth "does violence" to the Epistle
to the Romans and its author, and this violence does not affect
only this or that point, but "the very understanding of reality"
which Barth intends to convey. Bultmann said this was so
because Barth, despite his declarations of principle, did not take
seriously enough the letter of the Pauline *corpus,* its meanderings
and colorations, its "tensions" and "contradictions," its strong
and weak points. Thus, said Bultmann, to recognize the tenta-
tive character of the Pauline procedures—for example, the influence exercised on Paul by Jewish theology or Hellenistic
rationalism—is not necessarily to allow oneself to be imprisoned
in critical history or philology; but it is rather to eliminate the
risk of substituting one's own thought for the author's, and to
demonstrate "where and how the reality is expressed, so that I
may grasp this reality with certainty—a reality which is greater
than Paul himself." "And in this way," Bultmann continued,
"criticism will never be too radical"; it is a criticism which
"will clearly bring out the transcendence of that which the text
expresses in regard to itself and its author."

Four years later, Bultmann wrote another review, on Barth's
brief commentary on the First Epistle to the Corinthians. The
commentary was concerned mainly with Chapter 15, and was

entitled "The Resurrection of the Dead."[6] Bultmann's review was again largely in Barth's favor. He claimed to agree with Barth on a number of important points. Regarding one particularly important passage of the commentary, he said that he "admires the ability of Barth to grasp the main ideas of the text." He added, however, that he himself "would not be able to proceed in this way," for, he said, "it would necessitate, in my opinion, a more sustained exegetical effort and conceptual analysis to reach justified conclusions." Especially, he maintained, "several false interpretations would be avoided by the consideration of the historical situation."

Besides agreeing with Barth's explanation of many details in the epistle, Bultmann was even more in accord with Barth on the necessity and widespread concern for an exegesis which, not disdaining but surpassing a straight historical and philological analysis, would lead to a critique of the very thing to which a given document attests. However, Bultmann found that, even to this end, Barth might have been more exacting on the scientific level itself. Then his daring would have been the greater and his interpretation the more faithful. That is why, Bultmann remarked at the end of his review, "the work is not finished; instead, we find ourselves once again at a new starting point."

About the same time, Bultmann published an article on "Liberal Theology and the Recent Theological Movement."[7] In this article Bultmann advocated, and eloquently expounded, certain fundamental theses of dialectical theology. But at the same time he strongly insisted that the recent theological movement had not arisen as a rejection of previous works and a mere return to a more or less updated orthodoxy. Rather, the

6. Bultmann's article appeared in *Glauben und Verstehen* I, Tübingen, 1933, pp. 38–64.
7. Reprinted in *Glauben und Verstehen* I, pp. 1–25.

movement was characterized by a critical discussion of liberal theology, acknowledging and respecting the resolutions of that theology but at the same time disputing some of its presuppositions, its spirit, and in some measure its point of view, and contesting some of its conclusions. Still, wrote Bultmann, "it is no accident that the recent theological movement did not originate in orthodoxy, but precisely in liberal theology." Moreover, if liberal theology had put itself in a dilemma, it must then be acknowledged—so Bultmann—that "more than one of these liberal theologians were under the influence of motives which led them to surpass themselves."

What liberal theology had failed to see was the relativity of some of the results of science. Its illusion (which betrays a lack of faith) had been to think that it could attain *directly* to the world of faith. It allowed itself in many of its representatives to become involved in a sort of "pan-historicism," comparable to pantheism. But God is no more encountered in the complex of historical realities than he is in those of nature. God can never be a "datum," and he is no more directly accessible to the historian or to the philosopher than he is to the physician or to the cosmologist. To encounter God, we may not avoid the *scandalon,* we may not be frugal with our faith, we may not, that is, shrink from allowing the Word of judgment and of salvation question us in our entirety, with all our science and all our research.

But just the same, Bultmann added, liberal theology has rendered immense services and made a contribution which cannot be taken away. The permanent achievement of this theology lies not only in the superb scientific work it accomplished, but also in the critical standards it developed. On this point, it rendered to education a service of great value, for it was an education "unto freedom and truth." Bultmann remarked that "we who are products of liberal theology could never have become or remained theologians had we not experienced in liberal theology the gravity of radical truthfulness. We felt the work of orthodox theology in the universities to be an exercise in compromise, in which we could have only a desultory existence." Moreover, when the new theological movement wants to remedy the shortcomings or delusions of liberal theology, Bultmann wrote, "there is no question of a *sacrificium intellectus* by which to abandon the consequent rational consideration of history." Nor, he continued, is it a question of skepticism, "of doubting the capacity of man's knowledge, of demeaning his reason, of simply giving up. Quite on the contrary: it is not so easy to speak of God that one can be content to designate him as the 'irrational.' In fact, one can never have too lofty a notion of reason, for it is when reason has been taken to its ultimate conclusion that it reaches the crucial point where it brings man face to face with the question of his own meaning."

In developing his remarks, Bultmann did not find it necessary to show his points of difference with Barth; he even cited Barth profusely to show the depth and soundness of the latter's insights. In insisting, nevertheless, on the undeniable value of scientific work and on the necessity of giving reason free rein to pursue its course, Bultmann had already framed the attitude in which he would see his own task as theologian and exegete. We find in these first reflections the outline of a hermeneutics whose nature and propositions he was unceasingly to define.

Thus from the outset Bultmann has *practiced* a hermeneutics. This is the very essence of his work, for he is first and foremost an exegete, and an exegete who thinks it necessary to reflect on his method in order better to fulfill his goal. As we have seen, Barth began his writing career with commentaries on Scripture. However, he very soon turned to the construction of a "Church dogmatics." Even his commentaries on Scripture are markedly of this "prophetical" stamp, for Barth is more concerned with preaching the word of God, with the sovereign liberty of one who is conscious of his transcendence in regard to any written text, than with patiently and laboriously deciphering it with all the available resources and in accord with the demands and standards of science. The Danish theologian N. A. Dahl, who is opposed to both attitudes, has written: "The difference in attitude which is apparent since the debate between Barth and Bultmann is due, at least in part, to the theological point of departure, which for Barth is the situation of the preacher and for Bultmann the situation of a hearer of the word."[8] Bultmann's reflection does not stem, as does Barth's, from a concern to rediscover the inspiration of the Reformers from reading Scripture. Bultmann's reflection developed out of the preoccupations of the professional exegete. It was provoked, first of all, by the attentive confrontation of a scholar with the New Testament texts, and by the difficulties that the exacting mind encounters in the effort correctly to understand the text and faithfully to translate it.

Likewise, the reflection of Bultmann, who has always been aware of the importance of questions of method, and never content blindly to follow conventional methods, has begun to be apparent in his technical work of exegesis.

Bultmann initiated his life work by writing a *History of the Synoptic Tradition,* which is the cornerstone of what came to be called the form-critical method, or more simply, form criticism. In the Preface to this work Bultmann avoids any digression on the method he thinks should be used in his study. Rather, he briefly shows the relation of his work to those of his masters, the exegetes of the end of the 19th and the beginning of the 20th century, and also to recent works of a similar inspiration as his own, such as Martin Dibelius's *Form Criticism of the*

8. See *Theologische Rundschau* 22, 1954, p. 23.

Gospels, and K. L. Schmidt's *The Framework of the History of Jesus.* With these authors Bultmann shared a concern for the *Sitz im Leben,* a concern, that is, for the text in relation to the living history which the documents describe, or, as he said in speaking of some Gospel pericopes, for "the point at which they appeared and were elaborated on in the community." However, he set his method, which is essentially "analytical" and "inductive," in opposition to Dibelius's, which is "deductive" and "constructive." This is to say that Bultmann did not examine the text in terms of an image of the history of the synoptic tradition which could be more or less *a priori,* but tried to depart from the text, with its diversity of elements, with the complex and original character it presents, in order to discover an image of the whole synoptic tradition in its history. We see here in Bultmann a kind of Barthian concern to let oneself be guided by the object of one's research. But Bultmann, far more so than Barth, located his object in the diversity of forms which yields to the analysis of the exegete.

In fact, the process recommended by Bultmann seemed to a number of exegetes and theologians to be rather "hyper-critical" (to use one of their expressions) and, in the final analysis, destructive, rather than capable of introducing us to the living meaning of the Gospel texts. This view stemmed from the fact that his critics were referring to a concept of faith and revelation different from that of Bultmann. Oscar Cullmann, who later was to become highly critical of the work of the Marbourg theologian, enthusiastically hailed the beginnings of this form criticism to which Bultmann had put the finishing touch. "It is strange," he wrote in 1925, "to see how the so-called liberal critics imagine a danger precisely where there is the greatest gain. It is true that the new method ruthlessly follows its scientific principle to the very end, but precisely in its final

conclusions it encounters an essentially religious point of view
. . ."[9] "The Protestant, having passed through the old critical
system characterized by the search for a historical kernel, no
longer adores God *in Christ,* but only attempts to worship God
as Christ adored him." "This, then, is the only remaining bond
between the Protestant and Christ . . ." "Is there no way to
solve this difficulty of modern Protestantism? Is it possible to
return to the Christ of faith without sacrificing scientific
sincerity? Perhaps the system known as form criticism is
destined to help us out of this impasse. . . . The attitude of form
criticism has not been dictated by some dogma. Rather, it is the
outcome of an effort of absolutely scientific sincerity, and it
seems to us that it is for this reason that the new system could
be called into play to render an immense service to Protestant
theology and the Protestant Church. It goes further than all the
old systems in admitting free research into the Gospels; nevertheless, because of it, the Christian can worship God in Christ."
In these well-articulated lines we find once again the meaning of
Bultmann's project—which is, moreover, akin to Barth's proposi-
tion in his Preface to *The Epistle to the Romans*—namely, the
rediscovery of the reality of faith at the extreme limit of the
scientific adventure, certainly not as the necessary result of this
adventure, but in the manner of a question raised by it and by
the inadequacy which has marked it. But this adventure is
Bultmann's very life, and he takes it much further than Barth
does: within this adventure, he thinks, he will have to face the
crucial decision for life or death. For him, this is the way that
the real decision of faith and the authentic encounter with the
word of salvation present themselves. Concern for scientific
accuracy and for the radical critical approach will always char-

9. "Les récentes études sur la formation de la tradition évangélique,"
in *Revue d'histoire et de philosophie religieuses* 5, 1925, p. 473.

acterize Bultmann's work, and from the midst of this concern he will pose the fundamental theological question: the problem of hermeneutics.

* * *

Bultmann dealt even more directly with the problem of hermeneutics in the Preface to his second important work, a slim volume entitled *Jesus and the Word*.[10] Here again, in a book destined for a large public, fairly original in scope, and rather wide in scope, Bultmann presented a brief manifesto of hermeneutics.

The Jesus that Bultmann here considered is clearly the Jesus of the Gospel, and none other. Bultmann indicated that he did not intend to speak of Jesus as the theologians, mystics, and spiritual writers over the years have been able to understand him and preach him. This Jesus is to be found only by direct contact with the Gospel texts. In other words, this is the Jesus which the faithful and exacting research of the exegete allows us to encounter. This image of Jesus would be in a sense the fruit of an authentic hermeneutics, and this fruit should in turn allow us to realize the soundness and fecundity of the hermeneutics.

In this Preface Bultmann thus brilliantly showed how he had examined the Gospels in order to present this Jesus to the reader. He subtitled his exposition "The Method of Consideration." But he immediately remarked that the word "consideration" is inappropriate. For, he continued, "one fundamental presupposition in the following pages will be that man cannot, if he wishes to grasp the essential, 'consider' history in the same way that he considers nature, the world around him, and in making

10. New York, 1958.

such a consideration, orients himself in relation to them."
Indeed, man stands in opposition to nature, whereas he cannot
consider history without at the same time including himself in
its course. Likewise is it impossible for him even to speak of
history without at the same time in some way speaking of himself. "Thus," says Bultmann, "man cannot objectively consider
history in this sense, as he objectively considers nature." For
this reason, the exposition which Bultmann gives in his *Jesus*
"should be more than an attempt to orientate the reader to the
interesting things of the past, more than a stroll through
antiquity. Rather, it should lead truly to an image of Jesus as a
part of our own history, in which we have existence, or to which
we have access to existence through critical research. In other
words, the exposition can only be a continuous dialogue with
history."

Bultmann insists that this dialogue is far more than a
dilettante's pastime. It consists in a man's allowing himself to be
questioned, to be put in question, by history. And this "being
put in question" does not involve just one specific part of his
existence, but involves him entirely—including even the method
of his own questioning. In his research he must be ready to
recognize the authority of the history with which he has undertaken dialogue. "That is why," Bultmann explains, "the examination of history does not result in a complete relativism, as
though the image of history were entirely dependent on the
relative point of view of him who considers it. Quite on the
contrary, it is here—if history is to speak truthfully—that
the researcher must abandon all that is relative, all the prejudices
that he carries with him, and which are the product of his time,
his formation, his own individual attitude." What is needed now
is not the attitude of the disinterested onlooker, nor is it so-
called scientific "neutrality." In order to see history as it is,

objectively (in the true sense of the word), it is important, rather, that he who approaches history not fail to question it in order really to learn something from it.

The objectivity achieved through a simple game of method consists, at best, in the researcher's freeing himself from subjectivity. But there will always remain the subjectivity involved in the method itself, that is, the partiality of viewpoint that the particular method necessarily represents.

Purely scientific analysis is certainly indispensable, and yet it is basically insufficient. Quantitatively, it can bring to light much that is new, but with regard to our specific concern, namely, man and his history, it does not give us anything really new, at least nothing that history does not already know in principle through its own research.

The limits of the purely scientific method are apparent, for instance, in the attempts at interpretation or psychological explanation of historical personalities or phenomena. These endeavors necessarily start from a certain conception of human psychology and its possibilities. It is a matter, then, of fitting the case in question into the universal categories of science. If this cannot be done, one simply concludes that the phenomenon envisaged is not answerable to history. The question is solely to know whether it is possible truly to "encounter" history. It is precisely this question which challenges anyone who believes that "the possibilities of his existence are revealed exclusively through history." Such, indeed, is Bultmann's fundamental conviction in his little book on Jesus. Therefore, he tries to bring the reader not so much to a consideration of history as to an encounter with it. Such an undertaking could only be realized by the presentation of his own encounter with history. It is for the reader to decide, in his turn, whether to remain at the distant level of consideration, or to attempt to approach the deeper level of encounter. This supposes a commitment which depends on personal decision.

Bultmann insists, however, on the essential though paradoxical connection between this personal commitment and the attainment of true objectivity. For it is this personal commitment which helps us to avoid judging historical phenomena by extra-historical norms, and introduces us to the very heart of history. It frees us from the false distinction between the "historical" and the "supra-historical."[11] Without doubt, explains Bultmann, if we want to see in the historical phenomenon nothing but data to be arranged in chronological order, we will easily find reason to evoke something "supra-historical" in history to justify our interest in it. But if we do this, we will surely miss what is essential in history, for that which is essential to an event cannot, by definition, be supra-historical, but must on the contrary be a temporal event.

The Jesus whom Bultmann presents to us is not, in the author's own words, "a great man, a genius, or a hero. He appears neither as demoniac nor as captivating; his sayings are not characterized as profound, nor his faith as mighty, nor his nature as artless. Neither is there question of the eternal values of his message, of his discovery of the metaphyscial depths of the human soul, and the like. Instead, the attention focuses on his will, which can consequently become present reality, as a function of his historical existence."

For the same reason, Bultmann does not examine the "personality" of Jesus; and this not merely by way of making a

11. In the same year, 1926, Bultmann wrote an entire article on the work of Dibelius. Entitled "Geschichtliche und übergeschichtliche Religion im Christentum," it appeared in *Glauben und Verstehen* I, pp. 65–84. In a short Postface to *Jesus and the Word* he also refers to the work of Dibelius, noting that time does not permit him to deal more directly with it there.

virtue of necessity. Bultmann is certainly convinced that "we can know almost nothing of the life and personality of Jesus, since Christian sources on the subject are fragmentary and legendary, and other sources concerning Jesus do not exist." The attempts of liberal theology to trace the life and character of Jesus have cancelled each other, and Albert Schweitzer's *Quest of the Historical Jesus* has confirmed their failure. Even on the important question of messianic consciousness, opinion is greatly divided. Bultmann himself takes a negative position. He does not deal with the problem in his book, not, he says, "because there is nothing to be said on the subject, but because I consider the question irrelevant."

There are surely good reasons for being interested in the personalities of the great men of history, but this interest does not touch what they themselves had most at heart. As Bultmann says, these men "were interested not in their own personality, but in their work. Their work was not, for them, an expression of their personality, making it 'intelligible,' or giving it 'form.' Their work was something to which they were committed, a thing which they willed, to which they dedicated their lives."

In dealing with personages such as Jesus, whose most important action was their word, we can show their purpose only through their words, their thoughts, in short, their teaching. In this regard, it is important not to lose sight of the essentially historical character of this teaching, which is the expression of a living purpose. The teaching of the Jesus of the Gospels does not consist in an exposition of eternal truths, whose formulation would merely be a "recollection" in the Platonic sense—nor is this the purpose of his teaching. The historical significance of Jesus' thought (as opposed to its purely rationalistic significance) lies in the temporal act of its formulation. This significance can be understood only by the man who discovers in it the meaning of his own existence, an existence characterized by flux and by insecurity, an existence subject to its own decisions. "When we encounter the words of Jesus in history," warns Bultmann, "we are not to judge them on their rational validity by the norms of a philosophical system; we must rather let them question us as to how we want to understand our own existence. What is presupposed here is that we are troubled by the question of our existence. In this case, our research into history will lead not to the enrichment of timeless knowledge, but to an encounter with history, itself a temporal event. This will be a dialogue with history."

These remarks justify Bultmann's limited concern for drawing lines between the words which Jesus actually spoke and those which are to be attributed to the community which transmitted his message. Bultmann treated of this latter problem more directly in his *History of the Synoptic Tradition,* whose principal conclusions he presupposes are known, and to which he refers the more demanding reader on this point. However, since his purpose is to confront the reader with a living message and the historical movement connected with it, the identity of the bearer of this message is for him of minor importance. We may even, asserts Bultmann, place the name of Jesus in quotation marks. For the historical phenomenon to which this name refers would remain unchanged, and it is this phenomenon alone that concerns us, and renders us problematic by revealing new possibilities.

We may compare this last remark with one which Henri Bergson makes in his *The Two Sources of Morality and Religion.* In treating of Christian mysticism and its transcendence, he notes that this creative current which flows through humanity must have had a beginning. Since it is essentially personalist and personalizing, Christian mysticism could not but have a personal origin. Indeed, Bergson adds, "at the origin of Christianity there is Christ." He does not intend to go into a discussion of historical criticism. Still, he specifies, "From our standpoint, which shows us the divinity of all men, it matters little whether or no Christ be called a man. It does not even matter that he be called Christ. Those who have gone so far as to deny the existence of Jesus cannot prevent the Sermon on the Mount from being in the Gospels, with other divine sayings. Bestow what name you like on their author, there is no denying that there was one. The raising of such a problem does not concern us here. Let us merely say that, if the great mystics are indeed such as we have described them, they are the imitators, and original but incomplete continuators of what the Christ of the Gospels was completely."[12]

Bultmann and Bergson indeed move in fairly different worlds of thought. Bergson sees mysticism as the essence of Christianity. Bultmann, on the other hand, like most modern Protestants, feels that all mysticism is suspect from the point of view of Christian faith. For him, mysticism is a thing of man, whereas faith is beyond all human possibility, created entirely by the historical and gratuitous word of God. Without doubt, this difference of thought stems from a conflict of terms, as so often happens. According to Bergson, Christian mysticism postulates the free intervention of the God of love. Bultmann and Bergson, in different terms (and some of Bultmann's are unacceptable[13]), both propose an interpretation of Christianity as a living and personal appeal to the freedom and generosity of man, an appeal which opens up to that man new possibilities, or rather, the world of the impossible: the divine.

12. New York, 1954, pp. 239f.
13. This is particularly true when he doubts the historical validity of the Gospel data, and separates the message from the person of Jesus much more than does Bergson.

CHAPTER THREE

The Principle of Existential Interpretation

DEMYTHOLOGIZATION
AND EXISTENTIAL INTERPRETATION

THE CONCEPT of demythologization is central to the thought of Bultmann. In fact, for Bultmann, demythologization is the only possible approach to the problem of New Testament hermeneutics as it appears and must be resolved today. In discussing his manifesto *The New Testament and Mythology*[1] with Karl Jaspers, Bultmann wrote, "The real problem, then, is the problem of hermeneutics, that is, of the interpretation of the Bible and of the Church's preaching so that they may be understood as words addressed to man. It seems to me that, despite his lengthy discourse on comprehension, Jaspers has not fully grasped the problem of hermeneutics. Obviously, he cannot be blamed for not having himself had the experience of interpreting a biblical text. But may we not rightfully expect him to try to understand this task and the responsibility it implies?"[2]

It is now for us to examine Bultmann's basic preoccupation with this original position on the problem of hermeneutics, and

1. Reprinted in *Kerygma and Myth* I, New York 1961.
2. *Kerygma and Myth* III, p. 51. See also *ibid.*, II, p. 191.

particularly to grasp the precise meaning of the solution which Bultmann outlines immediately after formulating the problem. What he does first of all is to take a courageous look at the New Testament just as it appears to us, and faithfully to estimate the difficulty which its reading presents to modern man.

Bultmann summarizes the findings of his examination as follows: The world view which the New Testament unceasingly refers to, its whole system of representation, the entire world which produced its authors, all these are rooted in myth, a mode of thought marked by confusion, indeed by incoherence. For Bultmann, "mythology is a way of expression by which what is not of this world, the divine, appears to be of the world, human; the beyond appears as the here below. According to this way of thinking, the transcendence of God is seen as a matter of spatial remoteness, and worship as a material action releasing non-material forces."[3] According to Bultmann, mythological thought is diametrically opposed to scientific thought, which is characterized by the principle of determinism, that is, the coherence of a universe governed by laws. Now, scientific thought has irrevocably become our way of thought, and so it is, strictly speaking, impossible for us to adhere to the New Testament world view.

To expose in all its gravity and urgency the problem raised by this state of affairs, Bultmann emphasizes that he is not concerned merely with this or that problematical detail of the New Testament. A world view does not simply detail a number of images relative to objects of our experience. Rather, a world view somehow informs, *a priori,* this whole experience; and it stems from a determined "self-comprehension," from the fundamental understanding that we have of ourselves in relation to the world and to God. Thus the task of hermeneutics does not consist, for

3. *Ibid.,* I, p. 22n

Bultmann, in the mere selection of scriptural elements to be retained or rejected. "The mythical world view," he insists, "can only be accepted or rejected in its entirety."[4]

At the same time, Bultmann considers hermeneutics as anything but a negative enterprise. The critique of biblical data that he envisages "does not consist in the elimination of mythological statements but in their interpretation." Biblical criticism, he goes on to specify, "is not a process of elimination but a method of hermeneutics" —in the most positive sense of that word.[5]

If Bultmann can have given us the impression that he took some real pleasure in bringing to light and even magnifying those New Testament data which would be shocking in some aspects to modern man, this does not diminish his purpose, which is to rediscover, by earnest effort, the witness of the biblical texts. For he believes that the actual message has little to do with the form under which it has been communicated to us. Bultmann here has no thought of "saving" the New Testament, or anything of its content, in the course of this movement which seems to reach beyond the horizons of contemporary man. His main intention is essentially to be faithful to the New Testament, and to translate for the modern world this message which he sees as real, as actual.

The New Testament does not purpose to give us a world view, but to give us a message, a living word bound only accidentally to the representational world in which it was formulated. To discover and express this message should be the objective of every exegete who wants to be faithful to his purpose as well as to himself and to those for whose benefit he undertakes his task. And this is the positive and the most important

4. *Ibid.*, I, p. 21.
5. *Ibid.*, II, p. 185.

aspect of Bultmann's work; more precisely, to establish the method, the process by which we can come to an understanding of what the New Testament has to say, and by the same token faithfully to express it.

Bultmann is not, properly speaking, defining a new problem, but merely resuming the old and fundamental problem of hermeneutics in terms which seem more adequate to him. That he is aware of this fact was made clear during a famous conference on demythologization, when he took care to recall summarily—if perhaps a little too hastily and too simply—the "previous attempts at demythologization," especially allegorical exegesis and the exegesis of the old school of liberal theology.[6]

* * *

The positive solution which Bultmann brought to the problem of New Testament hermeneutics is that of existential interpretation. Having evinced the "mythical" character of most of the New Testament data, Bultmann emphasized that "the myth does not require a cosmological interpretation but an anthropological, or rather an existential one."[7] What does all this mean for man? What does all this mean for my existence? These are, in other words, the questions which must be considered in face of the disconcerting data of the New Testament. "In the mythology of the New Testament," Bultmann explains, "it is not the objective content of the representations considered in itself which has to be studied, but the understanding of the existence which is expressed in the representations."[8]

In what precisely does this hermeneutical process consist, this

6. See *ibid.,* I, pp. 22–26.
7. *Ibid.,* I, p. 22.
8. *Ibid.,* I, p. 23.

process which Bultmann favors, and which he characterizes as existential interpretation? In trying to answer this question, we will come straight to the heart of Bultmann's undertaking, and at the same time we will discover what is giving direction to most of the current reflection and discussion on the hermeneutical problem.

It is important to note, first of all, that by using this principle, Bultmann intended to take up again and to evaluate some of the most basic insights of dialectical theology. At a conference held in 1927, on the "Significance of Dialectical Theology for New Testament Science,"[9] he pointed out that "the key notion of dialectical theology is to take into consideration the historicity of the human being." To take into consideration the historicity of the human being means never to undertake an investigation without recalling that we are challenged by it; and that this investigation reveals to us not only new realities but also new *possibilities* for our existence.

This consideration is especially necessary since the undertaking to which we are dedicated is to be a theological one. Paradoxically, it is the only way to safeguard the transcendence of that which our language aims to express. It is all the more necessary to make this remark when we begin to explain the nature of existential interpretation, since such interpretation is all too easily labelled as anthropocentric. Bultmann feels that we respect the transcendence of God not by disregarding man, but rather by never losing sight of him, who in his language and in all his theological undertakings remains under the judgment of God.

In an article entitled "What Does It Mean to Speak of God?",[10] Bultmann explained especially that one can never speak *about*

9. Reprinted in *Glauben und Verstechen* I, pp. 114–133.
10. In *Ibid.*, I, pp. 26–37.

God but only *of* him. For, in Bultmann's words, "this cannot be done from a point exterior to God; and one cannot, therefore, speak of him by repeating universal propositions and formulas whose truth would be irrelevant to the concrete existential situation at hand." In other words, "If one wants to speak of God, it is obviously necessary to speak of oneself."

In order to understand what is meant by existential interpretation, which attempts to meet the fundamental need for a real theological language, it is important to note that the "existence" referred to is not to be confused with a limited and too immediate "subjectivity." Existential interpretation will by no means consist in fitting the data of Scripture into the domain of our soul or of our inner experience. The existence in question is, in fact, so Bultmann, "something as singular as God himself. We can no more speak about it than we can speak about him; we can no more control it than we can control God." We can speak about neither one because we cannot really detach ourselves from them, we cannot escape them. And yet at the same time, and for the same reason, we are always talking about our existence (and perhaps God's too). The authors of the New Testament could not, any more than we ourselves, escape the condition of man and of the language by which he expresses himself. Awareness of this fundamental fact and concern for drawing out all its conclusions: this is the prime reason for an existential interpretation.

Finally, it is necessary to add that Bultmann finds in the New Testament more than one point of reference to the only way of speaking of God that seems to him acceptable. In the book whose Preface was analyzed in the preceding chapter, he says that for Jesus "there does not exist anything like *divine nature.* Such an idea is specifically hellenistic. For Jesus, God is the power which puts man in the way of decision, which confronts him with the demand for the good, which determines his future. Therefore, God cannot be regarded *objectively* as a nature subsisting in itself. It is only in the real comprehension of his own existence that man can reach God. If he does not find him there, he will not find him anywhere else.[11] Bultmann went on to say that "Jesus speaks of God only to assert that man is claimed by God's will, and determined in his actual existence by God's demands, God's judgment, God's grace. Moreover, the far-off God is at the same time the God near at hand, and man does not grasp God's reality by fleeing his own concrete reality, but rather by holding fast to it. Jesus does not speak of God in abstract truths or in dogmatic utterances; he speaks only of what God is for man, and how he deals with him . . . One cannot speak of God as Jesus did except by speaking of God's activity . . . As the essence of man is found in his action, so is God present there where he acts. Thus Jesus does not introduce any new concept of God, nor any new revelations of his essence, but he does bring the message of God's will, the message of the kingdom to come. He speaks of God by speaking of man, and he shows that man is in the final hour of decision and that God has directed his sovereign call to man's will."[12]

However, existential interpretation is not based only on a number of obvious New Testament data. It also corresponds, according to Bultmann, to certain insights and demands of contemporary thought. The thorough examination it has wrought makes room for a systematic development of the existential viewpoint in the reading of the biblical texts, and for the expression of the existential meaning of these texts which seem, at first, to offer another viewpoint.

The meaning that we look for in words can usually be ex-

11. *Jesus and the Word,* p. 103.
12. *Ibid.,* pp. 151f.

pressed in certain very simple formulas: I love you; I hate you; you are forgiven. Nevertheless, the existential meaning of formulas used to express a thought is more often indirect. If the language of Jesus often manifests an undeniable existential character, many of the expressions and images of the New Testament, especially those suffused with mythology, reveal their existential meaning only through a process of interpretation which demands a certain technique. This technique was elaborated in especially precise terms by Martin Heidegger. His philosophy, particularly under the name of "existential analysis," furnished "the concepts which allow us to speak adequately of human existence."[13]

But Heidegger's philosophy offers more than a mere system of concepts. Or rather, this system expresses an entire understanding of man and reality, an understanding which can be put to use in the interpretation of texts. The fundamental principle of this anthropology, of this ontology, is that man's being is essentially historical, that is, evolving, choosing for itself and making itself, questioning itself, a problematic being, a "possibility." As Heidegger put it, "We think we understand more exactly than the idealist, the romantic, or the naturalist schools of thought the existence of man when we characterize it as a *historical* existence. By the historicity of the human being we wish to signify that man's being is '*potential* being.' Thus, the being of man is beyond his own control, it is challenged by every concrete situation of life, and it is realized through decisions in each of which man *does not choose anything for himself,* but chooses his own possibility."[14] The object of existential interpretation, which refers to this fundamental conception of human existence, is thus to express the Christian faith

13. See *Glauben und Verstehen* II, p. 232.
14. *Ibid.,* I, p. 118.

and the message in view of which it determines and formulates itself, in terms of this historicity of the human being as analyzed by Heidegger's philosophy.

Since he is a historical being, a potential being, a being which in some sense determines itself, man's being is essentially realized by action. Heidegger felt that the Christian conception of the human being, as well as that conception to which the modern philosophy of existence returns us, is this, that "by action, man conquers the true possibility of his being,"[15] and that "it is only in action that we are ourselves."[16] The organ of action is the will. It is through his will that man clarifies himself; the will is man's being (*Wesen*). We have already seen that it is because they *willed,* and because of their "work," that the great men of history are styled as such, and are interesting for us.

It is for this reason that existential interpretation, while faithful to the profoundest meaning of the texts it deals with, will always challenge whoever applies himself to it, or uses it to help make a decision. In the case of the biblical writings, this is a question of opting for or against faith.

We should beware of too hastily labeling as "voluntarist" this concept of man which is basic to existential interpretation. The decision in question, the act of will by which existence is realized, always communicates a certain "comprehension" of reality. It is always in a certain "understanding" that existence is expressed and increased. Existence is never given, nor is it effectively realized without a "comprehension" of existence. The acceptance or rejection of faith, although it is not the result of rational demonstration, ought no less to be a human decision, a "comprehending" decision.[17] What existential interpretation

15. *Ibid.,* I, p. 240.
16. *Ibid.,* I, p. 34.
17. See *Kerygma and Myth* I, p. 46.

aims at is the coincidence of the "act of thought" and the "act of life."[18] This coincidence alone allows thought to be genuine, that is, not to be lost in its representations but to retain the meaning it expresses, and at the same time it allows the existential subject to make a decision in freedom.

This interpretation, while it is concerned with corresponding to life, with calling forth a practical decision, with meeting the living word and the absolute standards of faith, nevertheless strives to remain in its own sphere, namely, that of explanation, of manifestation, of encounter. It does not in any way want to force a personal decision, much less act as a substitute for such a decision. Rather, this interpretation allows a decision to be made open-eyed, in full responsibility, while still resting solely on itself. To understand this paradox it is important fully to understand the distinction, fundamental for Bultmann, between "existentialist" and "existential." Bultmann feels that many of the objections raised against him hinge on a failure to see the basic difference between the two orders to which these terms refer.

The distinction itself is clear, whatever its value. The existentialist order refers to a purely formal or structural viewpoint; the existential, on the other hand, refers to effective, concrete realization. The existentialist viewpoint corresponds to the general structures inherent in every existence; the existential to the singular form which an existing being gives concretely, here and now, to his own existence.

In existentialist interpretation the exegete does not intend to make of his work a profession of faith or of incredulousness (this would rather be of the existential order). He means, instead, to examine the text and interpret it in terms of the

18. See *ibid.*, II, p. 188, and *Theology of the New Testament,* New York, 1951 (vol. I) and 1955 (vol. II).

universal structures of existence, which reflection, to some extent, can establish *a priori;* only amid these structures can the text reveal its meaning. In other words, the existentialist interpretation is *a priori* concerned with the possibility of an exegesis which is meaningful for existence, that is, which discovers its ultimate meaning. The existentialist interpretation defines a hermeneutics which, in order not to stop half way in the quest for the meaning of the texts, measures itself against and joins itself to that fundamental hermeneutics which for Heidegger constitutes the phenomenology of *Dasein.*[19]

If the existentialist interpretation refers to "norms," these are in no way dogmatic or moral imperatives which might be coercive to the will of the one who devotes himself to it when he examines the text or appropriates the results that this interpretation was able to produce. The norms in question are none other than the norms of intelligibility. As such, they enlarge the field of freedom, and emphasize the fact that existential behavior springs from freedom alone. Thus, in Bultmann's own example, the existentialist interpretation of love will establish norms for love only in the sense that it will define the general conditions to which all human conduct ought to respond if it is to be inspired by love. However, it will not go so far as to indicate "how I must understand my love *each time.*" Rather, says Bultmann, "the existentialist analysis can only make me see that each concrete instance of love can only be understood existentially, and that I cannot be deprived of my decision by any existential analysis."[20]

Rigorous analysis on the level of intelligibility, seeking the final, axial meaning of texts without imposing a practical meaning on them, calls forth an existential decision which, in view

19. See above, p. 23.
20. *Kerygma and Myth* II, p. 194.

of the biblical texts, will bring about, according to Bultmann, a choice between deadly self-sufficiency or faith which opens the way to future life: such is the nature of the existentialist interpretation. Still, although Bultmann's hermeneutical project immediately attracted a good number of exegetes and theologians, it has also met with hesitancy, and aroused intense disquiet and severe criticism.

THE CONTROVERSY OVER "PRELIMINARY COMPREHENSION"

Karl Barth has on several occasions vigorously opposed the hermeneutical thesis of Rudolf Bultmann. Barth does not hesitate to note his points of agreement with Bultmann. We have already indicated these points: emphasis on kerygma and concern for the living word. Barth recognizes "specifically Pauline accents" in Bultmann's account of the Christian faith. He does not reproach Bultmann for borrowing from the language of the philosophers, for it is hardly possible to do otherwise. "There is some philosophical terminology in the theological language of each of us," he wrote. He further recognizes that all contemporary theologians are more or less inclined to "think and speak about existentialism."

All the same, Barth feels that Bultmann gives pride of place to what should always be secondary and subordinate; he continually deplores Bultmann's misplaced emphasis, indeed his drastic inversion of perspective. Bultmann's first concern, in fact, is the receptive subject, his comprehension, and the interpretation given him with this end in view. His concern is not—as Barth feels it ought to be—for the reality to be interpreted. Thus the category of myth, which Bultmann uses to present his problem, represents a norm which is foreign to the New Testament texts, and which is better suited for describing what modern man understands by myth.

It is not surprising, then, that Bultmann presents an interpretation of the New Testament which reverses the order of things. The message of the New Testament does not primarily concern man, or the profit he derives from the message. Bultmann refers several times to the famous phrase of the young Melanchthon: "To know Christ is this: to know his kindness." But to make of this saying a principle of hermeneutics would, in Barth's words, be an "inversion, fraught with consequence, of the New Testament."

According to Barth, in fact, the salvific action of God is not something that is discovered "after the event, in the mirror of Christian existence." It is what is first of all announced in the appearance and the work of Jesus Christ. But it is precisely these events which, according to Bultmann, are measured by the significance they have for human existence. It is not so much Christ who is important, but the encounter with him. In the Christ event, Bultmann puts the emphasis on the event. As Barth remarked, "that Christ be (the object) of kerygma, this can certainly be obvious, but not the inverse: that kergyma be (the equivalent of) Christ." It is surely not fitting to separate Christology and soteriology, but in this unity, contrary to what is found with Bultmann, Christology comes first, and is the foundation for soteriology. For Jesus Christ is greater than our faith, he precedes it, he arouses it by triumphing from the outset over our incredulousness, and by subsisting independently of its vicissitudes. Bultmann's interpretation is under serious threat of Docetism: the Jesus of the synoptics is scarcely considered, and the Old Testament is practically left aside. Indeed, this interpretation might end by again turning the Gospel into law, with man's actions becoming the determining factor, and with faith identifying with an "imitation of Christ" along the perspective of the old liberal theology.

There must surely have been many reasons which led Bultmann to this method of interpreting the New Testament. Barth suggests these: a rationalist heritage marked by the Marbourg cult of accuracy; an apologetic concern, analogous to that of Schleiermacher, in the presence of the cultivated mind; a historicist formation in the sense of the nineteenth century tradition; a Lutheranism with its clearly anthropocentric orientation; and, finally, an intoxication with the new philosophical *eureka* of which the history of theology furnishes more than one example.

Barth feels that all these factors figure in the concern for comprehension which animates Bultmann, and which it is, therefore, important to examine. What is meant by "comprehension" of the New Testament? Or, more generally, what is the meaning of the verb "to comprehend" in Bultmann's hermeneutics?

Barth effectively concentrates his criticism on the principle of existentialist interpretation, and especially on the idea of a necessary "preliminary comprehension." He is aware that this process of existentialist interpretation, proposed by Bultmann, has been illuminating for many theologians, who have seen in it a principle of reconciliation between the concern for scientific rigor and effective preaching, and have recognized in it certain accents of Luther. But what Barth finds more than questionable is precisely this marvelous concordance, these "simplifications and concentrations" of Christian reality that delight the spirit and captivate the will. Barth does not concede that the New Testament is to be approached in terms of a preliminary comprehension drawn from a particular philosophy. The primacy accorded this comprehension could not, even under the present circumstances, ground itself on the undeniably representational character of the philosophy advocated, as if modern man were incapable of expressing himself in another language.

How, then, is the key to the true understanding of the New Testament to be found in existentialism? Barth sees in it rather an obstacle to the true understanding of the content of the texts. The preliminary comprehension that this philosophy tries *a priori* to define, is actually an armor, as it were, cutting us off from any fresh understanding of ourselves, and from the entire reality of the New Testament.

We will never comprehend the New Testament if we think that we know beforehand what we can comprehend, if we barricade ourselves within the supposed limits of our ability to comprehend. For to comprehend the New Testament implies "a believing comprehension of the word of God, which is there attested to." Now, this word of God, so far from letting itself be enclosed in our natural capacity for knowledge, instead contradicts it, in the sense that it reveals to us unsuspected possibilities. To be sure, we always approach the New Testament with a certain preliminary comprehension of what we think possible, right, or important. To be sure, we always tend to want to "domesticate" the New Testament. But must we raise this unfortunate tendency to the rank of principle, of ideal method? Would it not be better, as Barth put it, "to allow the text of the New Testament to act as catalyst for its own comprehensibility, instead of using what is usually regarded as the proper faculty of understanding as the catalyst for the New Testament texts?"

All things considered, what Barth reproaches Bultmann with, and which cannot fail to affect him deeply as well, is that Bultmann returned to the point from which they had both originally set out, together with the other dialectic theologians, when they had undertaken the project which was to regenerate faith and evangelical theology. Barth had no desire to establish the law by which they were then bound as an over-all principle.

* * *

Barth certainly felt the formidable narrowness and grave insufficiencies of Bultmann's hermeneutical project. He clearly saw what was at stake, and could not bring himself to agree. His objections are not all equally convincing, and do not always seem to hit the mark accurately. In any case, Bultmann has no difficulty in showing that the preliminary comprehension to which he refers is something other than the "armor" which Barth feared, and that his own philosophy of existence does not occupy the dominant place which Barth denounces. Bultmann has justified himself on this score in a number of articles bearing directly on the subject at hand. In each of these articles, he develops the same basic insight, which we may now examine step by step.

First of all, we must grasp the necessity and the true nature of the preliminary comprehension of which he treats. All textual interpretation depends on how the text is questioned. If nothing is asked, the text can only remain mute.[21] In other words, all interpretation presupposes a living relation between the interpreter and his object. This living relation can, of its very nature, be very diverse. It may be determined by the external character of the text (which might be a mathematical treatise, or an imaginative tale, and so forth), or by an interest of the exegete himself (to gain knowledge of the historical background of the text, for example, or of its author). This interest will obviously

21. See *ibid.*, II, p. 191, and *Glauben und Verstehen* II, p. 228.

be rooted more or less deeply in the existence of the exegete; it will be, more or less, a question of life or death. And the deeper his interest in the text, the greater will be his expectation and his openness.

In the second place, we must determine in what sense we can speak of a presupposition necessary to any exegesis. It is obvious that serious exegesis must be free from prejudice. The results must never be determined *a priori*. Preliminary comprehension, which cannot be avoided, should not be visualized as a rigid framework which would limit at the outset what the text can convey. It can very well be the incentive for an ever more complete openness towards revelation. As the exegete deepens his examination, then, he will increasingly beware of any shade of bias.

In the third place, if the exegete refuses to be preoccupied by the terms of his exegesis, or to have any critical reflection on it, or to clarify the necessary preliminary comprehension, he is in extreme danger of making the most arbitrary and subjective interpretation. To scoff at philosophy is still to philosophize, and indeed, to allow the imposition of a bad philosophy. Bultmann recalled this fact to Karl Jaspers, who felt that a pastor knows better how to comment on Scripture than does an exegete who resorts to existentialist interpretation. Bultmann counters that if the pastor is to accomplish his task of interpretation, he must at least be able to understand the language in which the texts are written, and he will generally refer to other works. At any rate, his interpretation will never be purely pastoral, or accomplished exclusively in the name of faith. A certain amount of scientific and, possibly, philosophical thinking will always be inevitable. Jaspers undoubtedly has good reason to think that "the appropriation of biblical faith" and "a believing understanding" of the Christian message are not the fruit of scientific research. However, wrote Bultmann, "the appropriation of the biblical word through believing understanding is possible only when that word is translated into a language which can be understood today. But can such a translation be made without methodical research?"[22] Bultmann reiterates that there is certainly a prescientific understanding of Scripture, which can be a true "believing understanding." But this does not diminish the indispensable role which hermeneutical reflection ought to play, namely, "to throw light on this understanding and strengthen it, which means constantly to bring it back to itself, for faith is in constant danger of being misinterpreted in its own meaning—which is to comprehend the existential self—, and of being confused with the recognition of general truths and accepted dogmas. When prescientific, existential understanding of Scripture no longer exists and—as is the case today—is closed to most men, then [hermeneutical reflection] must begin by restoring the possibility for that understanding by destroying the misconceptions of it." Hermeneutical reflection is particularly important in our time since, according to Bultmann, "the understanding of Scripture has become uncertain and subject to discussion; preaching is either full of misconceptions or completely unintelligible; and the repetition of confessional formulas is thought to be the language of faith."[23]

Finally, in order completely to clarify Bultmann's basic insight, we must consider the application of preliminary comprehension to the particular interpretation of a biblical text. A living relation between the reader and his object, explains Bultmann, is no less necessary for the understanding of a biblical text in its right context than when the text is philosophical, literary, or artistic. In a sense, in fact, it is even more necessary,

22. *Kerygma and Myth* III, p. 53.
23. *Ibid.,* III, pp. 188f.

if it is true that the message of the biblical text, more than that of any other, is relevant for the reader. For it is a question here, not just of any light, but of the light which illumines his whole life. To think, however, that this living relation preëxists the enlightenment of revelation: is this not to destroy the gratuitousness of revelation by making it simply the result of the development of man's ability? Bultmann does not think so, for this relation exists only in the form of a sterile question referring to God, a question which is in some way basic to human existence, and which St. Augustine expressed in his well-known phrase in the *Confessions:* "You have made us for yourself, O Lord, and our hearts are restless until they rest in you." By examining or explaining this question, existential analysis does not develop, in the sense of showing forth, the potential of man; rather it can show that the question may not contain the answer. The more that critical analysis is conscious of what it represents, the more will it lay the foundation for the existential encounter with the text itself. It is even possible that the "question of God," which is often presented as the quest for salvation, the search for happiness, for true existence, will be recognized as an authentic question of God only in terms of revelation. The fact remains that, in causing us to examine this preliminary comprehension —which is, then, completely negative, and is implied in the question of God—, existential analysis deepens our interest in the biblical text, on the condition that we are concerned with our existence.[24]

* * *

Surely some of Barth's criticism of the idea of "preliminary comprehension" of biblical texts are not fully adequate. The con-

24. See *Glauben und Verstehen* II, pp. 231f., and also *Kerygma and Myth* II, p. 192.

cern of Bultmann to seek out and define a "true" philosophy[25] in broad outline in order to be able to conduct a valid exegesis; his recognition that in the heart of every man there is a call from God, however obscure; his concern to find a "point of encounter" with the word of revelation, even if he carefully defines in what sense this is to be taken,[26] all of this relates his position to that of Catholic theologians.

Although Barth's criticisms are not always adequate, his basic insights are valid. Bultmann approaches the New Testament in overly simple, rigid, and narrow terms. His concept of existence is rather vague. History and community, in the current sense, are almost entirely overlooked. This is also why—independently of what can be said of his unjustified and quite obsolete skepticism on the subject of the historical validity of Scripture— his message is weak and at times misunderstood.[27] If this weakness or distortion is to be effectively exposed, it is important at least to respect the fundamental concern which is at the root of his reflection on the hermeneutical problem, even if we do not accept all the terms of his problematics. We shall see in the final chapter how this concern is shared, although in different forms, by many Catholic intellectuals and scholars, so that it corresponds to some of the unavoidable questions of our time. Before doing so, however, we will hear the younger generation of Protestant theologians.

25. See *Kerygma and Myth* II, p. 192.
26. See the article "Anknüpfung und Widerspruch," in *Glauben und Verstehen* II, pp. 117–132.
27. For a critique which attempts to do justice to the positive aspect of the work of Bultmann, may we refer you to our *Bultmann et l'interprétation du Nouveau Testament,* Paris, 1963, especially pp. 62–71, 97–104, and 173–188.

CHAPTER FOUR

Current Research

GERHARD EBELING:
A THEOLOGY OF THE WORD

AMONG THE NEW generation of theologians following Barth and Bultmann, Gerhard Ebeling has perhaps the most original and profound reflection on the problem of hermeneutics. Although only in his early period of production, he has already published a work which allows us to consider him as one of the most important and representative theologians of our time.

This work treats of some of the most essential problems, and finds its source materials in some of the richest contributions of contemporary thought in philosophy, in history, and in theology. His work on the essence of the Christian faith, published in 1962,[1] is reminiscent of Harnack's work on a similar theme.[2] Both authors can certainly be considered as witnessing to a theological and religious era.

Harnack's work was situated in the idealist context of liberal theology, whereas Ebeling's presupposes the reaction of dialectical theology, his own understanding of the living word of reve-

1. *The Nature of Faith,* New York.
2. *What is Christianity?,* Magnolia, 1958.

lation and the decision of faith which responds to it, as well as the new horizons which were opened up by the philosophies of existence of our time.

Ebeling has continually looked to Luther for inspiration, and beyond the philosophers and the great theologians who immediately preceded him, especially Bultmann. A committed and perceptive return to the work of the great Reformers is a common characteristic of contemporary Protestant theology.[3] Ebeling himself began his research with studies on Luther's exegesis.[4] He is considered an expert on Lutheran theology, and was requested to submit the article on that subject for the third edition of the encyclopedia *Die Religion in Geschichte und Gegenwart*. His indebtedness to Luther is far from servile; rather, he is able to revive some of the basic insights and formulas of the Father of the Reformation. This ability to handle material in such a way, without affectation, without overdependence on current jargon, is characteristic of all of Ebeling's work. It has certainly contributed to his present success as a teacher at Zurich in the chair of Emile Brunner, after several years at Tübingen, and to the increasing popularity of his writings.

Contemporary thinkers have one thing in common with the Reformers: the importance they attribute to the word. The Reformers tried to evaluate the word of God as attested to in Scripture and preached by the Church, whereas contemporary philosophers are concerned with the word, with language, insofar as it is the very expression of man. The Reformers, however, tried to evaluate not only the word of God but also the

3. For example, the work of Karl Hull on Luther during the first two decades of the present century is well known.
4. See, for example, his thesis, *Evangelische Evangelienauslegung. Untersuchung zu Luthers Hermeneutik,* 1942.

faith which is its response. The German language clearly shows the word-faith relationship as one between two words, *Wort* and *Ant-wort*. For contemporary thinkers, too, the word is not a mere instrument which allows man to communicate, but is the locus of human existence, and within the word an entire universe, whose bounds cannot be stated *a priori,* is revealed and created.

Ebeling's theology is always developed around a consideration of the word taken in its deeper and wider sense. For instance, he gave the title *Word and Faith* to a very important collection of his own articles and conferences, published in 1963 shortly after his *The Nature of Faith* in which he develops his major ideas on a level which is, on the whole, a good deal more technical.[5] Through the two basic concepts of *Wort* and *Antwort,* Ebeling believes he can examine the meaning of all Christian reality and, by the same token, of all reality.

To understand the importance which Ebeling accords to the problem of hermeneutics, which for him, more than for many others, is the theological problem par excellence, it is important to grasp the wide perspective in which he situates the reality of the word.

If the word is the point from which all reality must be seen, then in Ebeling's estimation this reality is always of the historical order for man. Reality is always discovered, and even established, in the position one takes in relation to the world and to God. Man is "radically challenged," and discovers himself when he realizes that he is challenged, even if he cannot at once identify the challenger, and even if the challenge does no more than to make him aware of the need for getting his bearings. "Adam, where are you?", is a question which arises from the very fact of existence. Whether man hears this question as the voice of the

5. Philadelphia, 1963.

world or the voice of God, he nevertheless awakens to find himself in the universe of the word, a universe which is both problem and challenge, which seems to him to depend on his decision, his response, his *Ant-wort.*

We may ask whether, in his theology, Ebeling refers only to this word which somehow becomes identified with the appearance of human existence, or whether he refers also to the strictly theological concept of the word of God. If there is no distinction, it would obviously be difficult to discern—in spite of such biblical expressions he might use, as the phrase from Genesis cited above—just how his considerations differ from those which our contemporaries make on the strictly philosophical level in regard to existence and language. In that case, he would undoubtedly view the problem of hermeneutics from perspectives analogous to those of a Heidegger or a Paul Ricoeur.

The answer to this question requires considerable qualification and it will introduce us quite thoroughly to the thought of the author, letting us see all the implications and the great importance that the problem of hermeneutics has for him.

Ebeling decries any simplistic opposition of the sacred and the profane in such a way that they would be juxtaposed or set one above the other. God cannot be assigned a place alongside some other reality, for it is within reality itself that God must be discovered. In his *Ethics,* Dietrich Bonhoeffer states that "there are not two realities, but *only one reality,* and that is the reality of God manifest through Christ in the reality of the world." Ebeling makes this affirmation of Bonhoeffer's his own,[6] explaining that it is necessary to be on guard against the "danger of schizophrenia which has threatened modern Christianity so that faith and understanding of reality are cut off from each other, and so that one lives and thinks as a Christian

6. New York, 1965. See also *Word and Faith,* p. 156, n. 7.

in two entirely different ways, in the daily world of work and pleasure, and in the world of the religious representations of Sunday."[7]

Moreover, the word of God is in certain respects no different from any other word. It is not, "so to speak, a separate category of word, alongside the word spoken by men which we usually call word."[8] It is transmitted by the same organs as any other word, that is, by the realities of the world; and, like any other word, it has meaning and makes communication possible. What characterizes it is that it, and it alone, is the *word* in its fullest sense, and that in and through it alone, every other word finds its fulfillment and complete meaning.

Any word is more than a simple transmission of a static content of "ideas." It always implies a "meaning," and effective orientation to a goal; it "evokes" a reality which it causes to happen, which it communicates, and in which it participates. Now, what makes the word of God different is that it, and it alone, has the power of bringing all reality to its goal and of giving to everything its true and ultimate meaning. It is affirmation and fulfillment, *Zusage* par excellence. It alone expresses and allows expression of the truth of man and of all things. The word of God is in contrast with the word of man as the word of the *verax* with the word of the *mendax*.[9]

Man is enmeshed in falsehood, in illusion, in darkness. His world is truly meaningless, his existence without future and betrayed by death, so long as he has not heard the salvific word which saves him from the dominion of empty conceit, of sin and of death, and opens to him an unlimited universe of

7. *The Nature of Faith,* p. 149.
8. *Word and Faith,* p. 325.
9. In this regard, Ebeling cites Num. 23, 19; Ps. 116, 11, and Rom. 3, 4.

promise and hope. Moreover, "what is meant by the word of God can be understood only from the Gospel." More precisely, the word of God is that reality which effects the passage from Law to Gospel, that ever-renewed passover in which man and universe find their meaning and their fulfillment. "Law and Gospel," a cherished phrase in the Lutheran tradition, is for Ebeling the key to any understanding of the word of God, as well as any understanding of existence and reality. He feels that it is only in dialectical and historical perspectives that transcendence, the supernatural, the hereafter, can be spoken of.[10] Through the liberating and illuminative word of God, man in turn becomes capable of a true word. But he is successful only to the extent that he understands the question which leaps from the very fact of his existence: "Adam, where are you?" This question invites him to surrender himself to the God who promises him life. The only authentic word that man can pronounce is the word of faith.

In speaking of the word of faith, we must be on our guard against hearing a word made up of words otherwise unknown, transmitted by a special organ of the one who pronounces it, a set of well-defined "articles" to which the believer can give his assent as he would to a mathematical formula or a scientific theory. The word of God which arouses faith, to which faith is the response (*Ant-wort*), is more a source of light for man than merely a new object for his understanding, which would merely be added on to the rest of his knowledge. A source of light is not made to be looked at for itself (for in that case it would dazzle rather than illumine), but its purpose is to throw light on a reality at its source. Thus faith is a sharing in the light which clarifies my existence and everything belonging to it.

It is a theme of Ebeling's theology that when there is a quest-

10. See *Word and Faith*, pp. 318f.

tion of faith, there is a question of reality. If concrete reality is abandoned, then so is the domain of faith, for then its meaning is betrayed. It is only through faith, which opens to us an infinite future, that true historical existence is realized, that is, true human existence. Our true humanity is realized only in faith. This realization does not come about in some ethereal sphere, or in the silence of pure interiority, but in the midst of men, in the real world of our experience and action. It is this world which is the locus of religious existence. It is the field where the seed of faith falls and germinates (see Mt. 13, 38). Not only must the faith be propagated throughout the world, but if it loses the world, it loses its very object and becomes perverted in illusion or superstition. The word of faith, called forth by the word of God, is the fulfillment of the human word in which all reality finds its meaning.

This outline of some of the main themes of Ebeling's theological reflection gives us to understand that in posing the hermeneutical problem— the problem of interpreting the word —he does more than merely reflect on theoretical principles, or on practical rules for the interpretation of a text. The hermeneutics he defines concerns all manifestations of reality and involves a total understanding of human existence and faith.

THE WORD OF GOD AND HERMENEUTICS

Ebeling very often mentions hermeneutics explicitly in his writings because he sees it as the major problem of theology, and he has devoted to it an entire article entitled "Wort Gottes und Hermeneutik."[11] The subject of this work, he tells us, is representative of the current theological problematic. It is the

11. Reprinted in *Word and Faith*, pp. 305–332.

result not only of the movement launched by the Reformation with its insistence on God's word, but also of the critical concern for truth which is characteristic of modern time.

The Reformation, however, did not only concentrate attention on the reality of God's word. In fact, a genuine hermeneutical principle is discernible in its work. The principle of *sola Scriptura* should be understood less as an attempt to "reduce the number of sources of revelation" than as an effort to bring about a new approach to revelation, in other words, the formulation of a "hermeneutical thesis." For practical purposes, the *sola Scriptura* principle is identical with Luther's formula that Scripture is its own interpreter.

However, the hermeneutical significance of the Reformation was for a long time ignored, especially by orthodox Protestantism which purely and simply identified God's word with holy Scripture, while making the latter a static rule of faith which quickly developed in a whole fixed system of dogmatics.

At the same time, however, critical exegesis began its own work and followed its own course in a similar way. Thus, there was an entire period of theology characterized by an increasing tension between dogmatics and exegesis. The study of Scripture, by which the Reformers had wanted to encourage the worship of God's word, seemed instead to bring it to its ruin.

This was the state of affairs when dialectical theology reacted (with the well-known effect) to the illusions and dictatorial pretentions of the historico-critical method, for the purpose of reëvaluating the concept of the word of God, showing that it is not of the same order of things as science as such. Karl Barth, and later Rudolf Bultmann, with their own characteristic approaches which we have already seen, endeavored to show that the "thing" in question in the biblical texts does not depend entirely on critical analysis, but that it is necessary to determine the relationship between this "thing" and the data established by critical research. Thus, the problem of hermeneutics was presented in a new light. If the relationship of God's word and hermeneutics must always imply a certain tension, then we must be careful not to approach the relationship merely as two distinct terms, so that the development of the one would lead to the destruction of the other.

It is at this stage of development of the question that Ebeling introduced his own considerations. For him, the fundamental error of Protestant orthodoxy and, for that matter, of all orthodoxy, has been to consider the word of God apart from its actualization in preaching, to make it some sort of object instead of seeing it as a kind of impulse. This is the reason, moreover, why orthodoxy could not recognize the strictly theological importance of hermeneutics. For hermeneutics is precisely that which allows God's word truly to be a word, in other words to attain its meaning in the encounter with the one to whom it is addressed.

Orthodox thought feared that this human attempt at interpretation might diminish the transcendent authority of God's word. It did not want to see this authority dependent on a natural, secular process. Since, however, orthodoxy felt the urgency to find for the discipline of interpretation a proper place, it took refuge for a while behind the distinction between sacred and profane hermeneutics, and later between general and particular hermeneutics. This led to the compartmentalization of reality and of the different aspects of knowledge, the attempt to reserve an area where the work of hermeneutics had no right to penetrate, for that would be an undertaking foreign, if not opposed to the movement of faith.

The outlook on the problem was transformed from the moment when hermeneutics no longer appeared as the simple application of rules external to the reality with which it dealt, but as a way of contributing from within to the discovery of this reality. In Ebeling's opinion, Heidegger and Bultmann played a determinant role in bringing this about. For both of them—and Ebeling was determined to follow them—hermeneutics shows an affinity with reality which allows reality to express and even to realize its meaning. Or rather, it is the impulse by which reality manifests itself and effectively attains its purpose. It is less an effort to understand language than it is the search for the meaning of reality by means of language. "The primary phenomenon of comprehension is not comprehension *of* language but comprehension *through* language." The word itself has a "hermeneutical function."[12]

This is as true in regard to the word of God as it is in regard to any other word. The purpose of hermeneutics is to effectuate that the word of the past, preserved in documents, become the living word that leads us into the future, that is, that it become once more a real word, thus regaining its full meaning.

From these perspectives, in contrast to those which governed the old orthodoxy, hermeneutics does not obscure the word of God with norms of interpretation external to it and thus threatening to destroy it. On the contrary, hermeneutics is a matter of necessity any and every time the word-event is obstructed, that is, whenever the word is no longer understood as word. Its role is to coöperate in the work of the word. "The content and the object of hermeneutics is the word-event as such."[13]

To say that hermeneutics has the word-event as its content and its object is not to say that it is a formal enterprise having no intrinsic connection with its object, but on the contrary,

12. *Ibid.*, pp. 318f.
13. *Ibid.*, p. 319.

that it is identical with the very activity of history and of reality. In particular, it implies the universe of the word which is realized in it. Hermeneutics can be exercised only by a man who is already a part of the word, and through whom or in whom the word is spoken. Hermeneutics begins with the word in order to ensure its genuine realization. It is always *situated* in a history whose movement it expresses. For this reason, moreover, it is always effected in a sort of circular movement.[14] It implies the spoken word, a given and past reality, but it also restores the reality of this given, this past event; it confers on the materialized word, which finally becomes no more than a thing, its reality as word.

Within the Christian tradition, the exercise of hermeneutics is identical with theology and the preaching of the Church. But since the role of hermeneutics is to make the word of God live, to manifest its enlightening and transforming power in the concrete reality of history, because, as we have said, there are not two realities, and because God's word especially does not differ in essence from the words spoken by man himself. Thus, hermeneutics in the Christian tradition does not consist in the development of a mysterious language which eludes the laws of human language. If hermeneutics is the interpretation of the Christian universe of faith, it is the interpretation of human and historical reality as such. This is what Ebeling attempts to show more precisely when he repeats and comments on the famous appeal of Dietrich Bonhoeffer for a "non-religious interpretation of biblical concepts."[15]

The appeal for a "non-religious interpretation of biblical concepts" is inspired in principle by Barth's basic insight that Christianity is anything but a religion. Religion is, in fact, a

14. Ebeling speaks of the "hermeneutic circle": see *ibid.*, pp. 321f.
15. This is the subject of a long chapter in *Word and Faith*, pp. 98–161.

very human thing, a haven which man constructs or sets aside for himself in which he can solve the problem of his disturbed and threatened existence. As for Christianity, it is the gratuitious intervention of the living God who confounds reality, and even man's religious searching, in achieving the impossible, the justification of the sinner.

Thus, explains Ebeling, Bonhoeffer's appeal, which seems itself challenging, in fact only translates the challenging character of the very word of the God of revelation, of his intervention into our history through Jesus Christ. The first import of Bonhoeffer's "non-religious" interpretation is that it be a consistently "Christological interpretation."

The second import, closely bound up with the first, is that our interpretation of the biblical word of revelation be concrete. By "concrete interpretation," let us understand an interpretation which relates to our existence and which by that very fact is realized in terms of that through which our existence becomes intelligible—that is to say, our reason. "Non-religious" interpretation is inspired by "intellectual honesty," which consists in considering the meaning of faith in God's word at the center of the reality in which I live, where my reason is exercised, where my judgment and my word are pronounced.

Finally—by way of expressing the same idea in another way— "non-religious interpretation" is equivalent to an interpretation inspired by faith. Not he who believes or who thinks he believes but rather he who does not believe ought to be the criterion of the meaningfulness of our preaching of God's word. For faith is not the preserve of believers, but rather the movement which transforms reality by exposing its ultimate meaning. Therefore God's word, which is always the word of true conversion, ought to be addressed to the unbeliever. Preaching does not presuppose faith, but rather always seeks to arouse faith.

Thus, "the concept of non-religious interpretation was not fabricated for the purpose of loosening the reins of theological investigation but to tighten them; not that the traditional theological and biblical concepts could easily be thrown overboard, but actually to regain possession of them; not to be guilty of meaningless jargon, but to strive for new expression of God's word; not to set life against doctrine, action against thought, but truly to integrate life into doctrine, action into thought; not simply to make comprehension possible for the unbeliever, but rather to make true understanding possible for theologians themselves; not that we might proclaim the non-religious interpretation as gospel, but that, if it is the right thing, we might proclaim the Gospel by means of non-religious interpretation" (*op. cit.,* p. 128). There is no question here of a kind of panacea which would facilitate the work of interpretation by providing prefabricated solutions. Rather, the process of non-religious interpretation is an ever new adventure, an adventure involving both the suppleness and the exigencies of life.

We have seen how Ebeling insists on the necessity of developing a hermeneutics which can realize the unity of life and doctrine, of action and thought; we have also seen him object to a juxtaposition of a sacred and a profane hermeneutics, or a general and a particular hermeneutics. He also insists that practical, dogmatic, and historical theology be made to coincide, and he sees this confrontation realized in the "hermeneutical problematic" which he advocates.

This inference is already drawn in the two articles in *Wort und Glaube,* of which we have taken note, and Ebeling returns to it in the first two chapters of a recent book, *Theologie und Verkündigung.*[16]

As did hermeneutics at its beginning, historical theology at

16. Tübingen, 1962.

first appeared to be the rival, and even the enemy of dogmatic theology, for it tended to minimize the affirmations and challenge the authority of the latter. Historical theology is the victim of its own one-sidedness. It did not see that its lack of concern for up-dating its object could only result in missing its object entirely. Moreover, if dogmatic theology contents itself with the repetition of confessional formulas, it neglects its true function, which is to arouse and animate faith by showing the precise and strictly established meaning which the word of God, conveyed by tradition, assumes here and now for concrete existence and for human history.

Consequently, Ebeling feels that if the expressions "historical theology" and "dogmatic theology" are rightly understood, they appear redundant (*op. cit.*, pp. 10 and 12). Both are concerned with tradition, but tradition must be seen in its twofold aspect of *traditum* and *actus tradendi* (*ibid.*, p. 13). Theology cannot neglect either aspect, for it is the very bond which joins them. Such a concern requires honesty in critical research, seeing the *traditum* for what it is, and attempting to give expression to its complete meaning. The error of biblicism and of confessional dogmatism is that they wrest from theology its proper responsibility (*ibid.*, pp. 14–15).

This responsibility is implied in the effective and eloquent proclamation of God's word, and therefore the unity of historical theology and dogmatic theology, effected by hermeneutics in its deepest sense, is also the unity of scientific theology and practical theology, or if you will, the unity of the Church's preaching. "Theology without preaching," writes Ebeling "is empty, and preaching without theology is blind" (*op. cit.*, p. 9).

More precisely, we might identify practical theology with spiritual, ascetic, or mystical theology, although these terms are not part of Ebeling's vocabulary. However, as we have already seen, what he does insist upon is that a reference to existence is demanded of any hermeneutics which is mindful of its responsibility to God's word.[17] The "existence" is the vital totality at whose center is man's free decision, by which man orients himself in relation the world and to God, and from which springs the word which gives everything its meaning. In order to define more precisely the locus of existence, of historical reality, of the origin of God's word, and of the pronouncement of the true word of faith, Ebeling resorts to the concept of consciousness, which he admits to having borrowed from Luther. He does not use the term in the sense of the psychological consciousness of idealism; he is not speaking of *Bewusstsein* but of *Gewissen*— and this is not to be equated glibly with what is commonly called moral conscience. This consciousness of which Ebeling speaks is less *Instanz* than *Distanz;* it is an indicator of the discrepancy between what we are and what we are called to be; it is the channel of God's unceasing call and challenge. Consciousness is at the source of all our responsible action (*ver-ant-wortlich* = answerable for); it is the field of our activity, the very expression of our humanity. In consciousness, "man truly identifies himself"[18] and experiences the concrete encounter with God, with the world, and with his fellow man. In consciousness, the future appears in fact, the word of salvation is contained, and God himself is experienced.[19] Thus, any theology which must refer to consciousness understood in this sense, will always be a historical, dogmatic, and practical theology—or, as we have called it, a spiritual theology. For Ebeling, this reference to consciousness is not a mere secondary aspect of the theological effort identified, as we have seen, with hermeneutical research. *Ex-*

17. See *Wort Gottes und Hermeneutik,* p. 347.
18. *Word and Faith,* p. 417.
19. *Ibid.,* p. 422.

plicatio and *applicatio,* if rightly understood, are closely aligned.[20]
Reference to consciousness is so essential for Ebeling that he is
not afraid to say that "the principle of hermeneutics is man as
consciousness."[21]

CONFESSIONAL DIFFERENCES IN THE LIGHT
OF THE HERMENEUTICAL PROBLEM

If the problem of hermeneutics is the central, the essential problem of theology, we can easily see how it may enlighten our
understanding of the history of the Church, and in particular
how it may be found at the root of confessional divisions.
Ebeling has strongly underscored the intertwining of the confessional problem with the problem of hermeneutics.[22] He has
made a detailed analysis of the relation of the two in a long
article on the significance of the historico-critical method for
Protestant theology ("Die Bedeutung der historisch-kritischen
Methode für die protestantische Theologie und Kirche"),[23] and
in an opusculum entitled *Die Geschichtlichkeit der Kirche und
ihrer Verkündigung als theologisches Problem.*[24]

Ebeling's initial hypothesis is that the different periods in the
life of the Church, as well as the different confessions, are
characterized by the way in which they conceive of the relationship between historical revelation realized in Jesus Christ and
the manner in which this revelation is made actual in the
present. Specifically, Ebeling indicates, "Catholicism and Protestantism are distinguishable by the individual position each takes

20. *Ibid.,* p. 27.
21. *Ibid.,* p. 332.
22. See *Word and Faith,* p. 30n.
23. Reprinted in *ibid.,* pp. 17–61.
24. Tübingen, 1954.

in the matter of hermeneutics, and consequently by the individual position of each with regard to the relationship between revelation and history."[25]

According to Ebeling, Catholicism resolves the problem of this relationship by identifying, above all, revelation and the gift of grace accomplished in Jesus Christ with the ecclesial and sacramental system. In the sacramental act and in the different manifestations of the reality of the Church, Christ himself and his power are effectively present. The reality of the Church, as that of the sacrament, is composed as it were of two levels, the human, the visible, the historical on the one hand, and on the other the divine, the mysterious, the eternal. But the one is directly given in the other. The doctrine of *ex opere operato* efficiently translates this conception of a present relation with the divine source of grace. This same solution is found in the notion of the Church as the "incarnation continued," which allows Catholicism to associate conservatism with an equally radical evolutionism, since whatever the historical existence of the Church has brought forth tends immediately to assume a divine character, being considered as the "development" of what was originally revealed. Such a juxtaposition of the human and the divine—which comes before their identification one with the other—is in the tradition of the metaphysical Christology of the early Church, which affirmed the distinction of the two natures of Christ within the single person of the Word.

Protestantism did not immediately abandon this conception of the relation of the human to the divine, of man to the historical events of revelation and salvation. Particularly in view of the Bible, it was tempted to retain a dualistic vision of things. In the human words of the Bible, Protestantism thought to find,

25. *Die Geschichtlichkeit der Kirche . . .*, p. 91.

more or less directly, the sacred deposit of God's word, and did not delay in developing an orthodoxy which it found capable of yielding the true revelation of salvation. However, by focusing the entire work of salvation on the mysteries of word and faith, it laid the groundwork for a radical revolution with regard to the understanding of our revelation to salvific revelation. Luther in particular led Christianity on a totally new course by his insistence on the *viva vox evangelii,* on the necessity of encountering in the Bible "that which gives us Christ," and by that very fact of determining the fundamental character of the Law-Gospel relationship.

The advent of the historico-critical method in our day allows us to follow this course to the very end. When put to use by a theology aware of its responsibility to the living word, the historico-critical method permits us to put to work, openly and bluntly, the major principles of the Reformation—*sola fide, iustificatio impii, theologia crucis*—since it prevents us from seeing faith as originating in or depending on any material aspect of the world, and continually allows faith to be aroused by the word.[26] If the word is to be now as it was in the beginning, it must come through history to launch the believer on an adventure in historical existence: this is the hermeneutical adventure. Whereas Catholicism seeks the benefits of salvation and revelation in the repetition of the sacramental act and in conformity to an objective rule of faith found in a firmly established tradition and guaranteed by the magisterium, Protestantism—insofar as it is more or less loyal to itself—seeks these benefits in its commitment to the development of a radically critical hermeneutics which would allow the original and authentic

26. See *Word and Faith,* p. 60. See also *Die Geschichtlichkeit der Kirche . . .,* p. 62.

word to be spoken unceasingly in an ever new manner in human history.

We can readily admit that hermeneutics is necessarily at the root of confessional division, insofar as it determines the correct meaning of the data of faith. In referring to this, Ebeling seeks to bypass any superficial conflict in order to get at the heart of the matter. Even so, he is not entirely innocent of oversimplification. If, in his treatment of Catholic principles, he evokes certain nuances which it has been impossible for us to retain in our summary presentation of his thought, we must admit that he is dealing mainly with the schemata of theological manuals. For example, the recent discussions of a number of eminent Catholic theologians on the problem of the natural and the supernatural point up the complexities of Catholic doctrine, which is open to varied interpretation, and which in any case is not satisfied (as we might be led to think) with a mere juxtaposition of the two orders.[27] Furthermore, Catholic doctrine on the sacraments is not exhausted with the principle *ex opere operato*. The sacraments exercise their power by *signifying* that power. *Significando causant:* that is, the sacramental sign calls forth an impulse of the spirit, which perceives its meaning and appropriates it in faith. Likewise, the entire mystery of the Church, which is not an inert presence of God among men, so far from being an obstacle to personal, intelligent, and loving relationship between the believer and his Lord, continually promotes this relationship in assuring its authenticity.

For our part, in speaking of the basic options of Protestantism, we too should avoid oversimplification. In the proceeding chapters we have seen the great divergence among several theolo-

27. For example, Henri de Lubac, *Surnaturel,* Paris, 1946; Henri Rondet, *Gratia Christi,* Paris, 1948; Hans Urs von Balthasar, *Karl Barth,* Cologne, 1951; Karl Rahner, "Nature and Grace," in *Theology Today,* vol. I, Milwaukee, 1964.

gians equally anxious to be faithful to the principles of the
Reformation. However, if we must explicitate what seems to us
to limit the scope or compromise the result of their common
reflection on the hermeneutical problem, we would have to say
that it is their inadequate understanding of that mystery of the
Church and of that sacramental order which Ebeling specifically
evokes with regard to Catholicism. Faith in the Church and in
the sacraments, as we shall see, does not suppress the problem of
hermeneutics, but sets it immediately into a less abstract, a less
idealistic context. It is no longer a simple problem of the meaning of a particular word or progression of ideas, but of a word
incarnate which, from the very outset, is also a gesture and an
institution, and which never ceases to make itself known at
once in the thought, in the ritual practices, in the life, the witness, and the struggle and suffering of a historical community
raised up by the Spirit of God. The result, as we shall see, is an
original position with regard to the problem of hermeneutics,
whose implications and undeniable importance Ebeling can help
us better to understand.[28]

* * *

We have wished to bring to mind primarily the thought of
Gerhard Ebeling, not only because it seems to us to be of interest in itself, but also because it is representative of a whole
theological school. This "new theology," as it is sometimes called,
is stated today under one form or another in numerous German

28. For further reading on the theology of Ebeling, consult our article,
"Foi et Parole. La théologie de Gerhard Ebeling," in *Recherches de
science religieuse* 50, 1962, pp. 5–31. Peter Langsfeld gives a penetrating
analysis of the same subject in his *Ueberlieferung. Tradition und Schrift
in der evangelischen und katholischen Theologie der Gegenwart*, Pader-
born, 1960, pp. 94f. and 169–172.

theological theses. It inspires an important part of exegesis and is revealed more or less fortunately in many sermons.

If we owe to Ebeling the more remarkable contribution to the subject, we must nevertheless mention one or the other theologian who takes advantage of the same world of ideas, before citing several contemporary works which arise from an opposite thought.

Alongside Ebeling, Ernst Fuchs is generally cited as one of the masters of hermeneutic theology. Many will even consider him the hermeneutic theologian par excellence.

Fuchs has, in fact, published several works which deal explicitly with the hermeneutic problem. The first of these, *Hermeneutik,* appeared in 1954. In it, Fuchs outlines a body of seminary or course material from which the casual reader may not derive much benefit. Some preliminary works of Karl Barth, Martin Kähler, Wilhelm Hermann, or Rudolf Bultmann should serve to introduce a systematic study of the problem. In the second part of Fuchs's study, strictly exegetical analyses overlap in a curious manner with the most abstract speculations. The important questions, then, are merely pointed out rather than developed.

A more elaborate explanation of the problem is to be found in a second work of Fuchs, which collates a number of articles, courses, and conferences of the author, under the title *Zum hermeneutischen Problem in der Theologie. Die existentiale Interpretation.* The purpose of the author's reflections here is to permit us to recognize all that is involved in the hermeneutical problem, that is to say, in fact, the ultimate questions of theology and philosophy. For Fuchs, the "crises" more or less outside the Church generally do little more than express a deeper crisis which is often less noticeable, a crisis of theology, of understanding the human discourse preceding revelation. The concern of Fuchs is to surpass in particular the level on which relative discussions of demythologization generally come to rest, and thereby to release all the implications and the entire range of questions raised by Bultmann on the problem which is, properly speaking, a theological one.

Fuchs admits that today the urgent problem of demythologizing the New Testament is a philological one in the proper sense of the word, namely, an eminent problem of comparative languages. But, he adds, the question is whether the demands for demythologization can even approach the very core of a theological problem. For him, in fact, the true problem lies on the ontological level, and he may thus ask, "Is the human being made up of facts, or does he answer to a language?" From this point of view, the hermeneutic problem is the ultimate problem, because it is a problem of language, and "it is only language that allows or grants being, and therein, be-ing, and be-ing as being" ("erst die Sprache das Sein und in ihm das Seiende und das Seiende als Sein gewährt oder erlaubt").

Whatever may be the depth of some of his ideas, Fuchs seems nevertheless to have drawn special attention to certain dimensions of the hermeneutical problem. It is less certain that he has thrown much light on the problem.

More stimulating, it seems, have been and are still the reflections and discussions on the emphasis on the "canon within the canon." One may say, in general, that contemporary German Protestant theology is at opposite poles to fundamentalism. It distinguishes so sharply between word of God and Scripture that it rather risks removing all bonds other than accidental between the two; thus it does not fear to find, in the New Testament itself, important traces of primitive Catholicism in which Catholic theology may continue to find a biblical justification.

One of the exegetical theologians in the camp of Bultmann who has most eloquently emphasized the diversity, that is to say, the contradictions existing within the New Testament, is Ernst Käsemann. In a well-known article, "Bergründet der neutestamentliche Kanon die Einheit der Kirche?", he maintains that the canon, "as such, that is, in the form presented to the historian, rather produces the multiplicity of confessions," or again, that "the New Testament canon is not located between Judaism and early Catholicism, but provides a plan and a foundation for primitive early Catholicism and Judaism." Whence the necessity for a *diakrisis pneumatoon:* "In other words, and to express ourselves in the manner of the New Testament, we are forced to distinguish among the various spirits embodied in Scripture itself."

One-side insistence on this point of view could easily, to be sure, lead to *Enthusiasmus* and *Schwärmerei.* Käsemann is aware of this, and takes care to avoid such dangers, as well as that of *Synkretismus.* The latter consists in purely and simply juxtaposing the different theologies actually contained in the New Testament, without locating and organizing them in a unified perspective. This is a matter of preserving the link between Scripture and the evangelical freedom of the spirit. "Responsibility and freedom": this should be the twofold concern of the exegete. As Käsemann points out, this was already the hermeneutical problem of the Reformation in its dialectical determination of the relationship between Scripture and Gospel. It is this principle that the modern exegete ought to take up again.

The "canon within the canon," then, is the Gospel, a magnitude which cannot be identified with any intellectual pursuit. It is a living reality, transmitted by the preaching of the Church and extending to faith. Käsemann identifies it with the justification of the sinner.

Contemporary Protestant theologians are far from adopting this principle. To Hermann Diem, for example, it appears too formal and precise to be able to lead the exegete to the subjective and the arbitrary. Thus he rejects even the concept of the "canon within the canon." For him, the canon, in the form under which it offers itself to our faith, plays a fundamental role. It is on the very text of this scriptural canon that faith alone may rest, if it is not to be led of itself to construct or fatally to distort its object. Diem admits that the New Testament surely is not yet homogenous doctrine. The authors of the different books express themselves in a variety of situations and according to perspectives which are far from identical. For all that, Diem does not advocate an eclecticism which would require synthesizing practically all the viewpoints represented in the New Testament without any effort to find therein any kind of unity. This would be an artificial intellectual game. We ourselves must receive the New Testament in a given situation, and it is in the context of this situation that we must be called and must listen, while in principle still keeping the New Testament as canon of faith. Diem feels himself authorized to neglect, or at least to minimize certain elements which a Catholic, for example, would consider essential (such as, especially, the pastoral epistles). In other words, Diem's chief concern is to point out that faith is never equal to its object. And he is so convinced of this that he seems to resign himself quite easily to an always fragmentary realization of the concrete content of the word of God. For him, this word does not exist basically as a totality, except under the material form of the text of Scripture.

In an interesting article entitled "Der Frühkatholizismus im Neuen Testament als kontroverstheologisches Problem," Hans Küng develops the idea that the presence of different points of view in the New Testament ought to draw all the confessions to an authentic catholicity, that is to say, to the search for that *plenitude* which could truly justify this diversity. It is enough to remark here that, although Diem may be right to criticize what is too formal in the hermeneutic principle of theologians or exegetes such as Ernst Käsemann, he himself does not seem to have a clear hermeneutic principle of his own. Perhaps this stems from the fact that, despite his interesting ecclesiological considerations, he does not envision seriously enough the possibility of a median term between the objective text of Scripture and the always partial, limited, fragmentary interpretation of the faithful.

Heinrich Ott, in emphasizing the specific function of dogmatics, concerns himself with this median term. He maintains that dogmatics exercises a sort of vigilant office in the preaching of the Church, which can never at every moment transmit the totality of revealed truth, and that this dogmatics, already grafted onto this preaching, refers to its object, as the word of God testifies. Dogmatics "is located, in a certain sense, between the Bible and the actual preaching of the Church" and "receives the role of mediation characteristic of the theological enterprise." In a sense, then, dogmatics is the guardian of that *thing* which is the base and determinant of the faith of the Church and which its preaching intends to transmit. Moreover, the Church is the *Sitz im Leben* of dogmatics.

Heinrich Ott devotes a great deal of attention to the problem of hermeneutics, which is and remains an important one. He is concerned with the occurrence of human comprehension. But he challenges the dichotomy made by Fuchs, and in general by the theologians of demythologization, between theology and preaching, between doctrine and the life of faith. His concern is largely a "thinking about faith." And one can neither resolve, nor even correctly pose the question without understanding the function of dogmatics. Certainly, it is still necessary to determine the exact nature of dogmatics, and therefore of this Church, outside of which it is impossible to envision this dogmatics, of this Church which is its *Sitz im Leben.* The expansion of our problem which Ott brings about obviously leads his own reflection closer to those which are current in the Catholic Church. Nevertheless, we must finally mention one more work which, though still partly in a rudimentary stage, is one on which more and more attention is being focused. It deals, in fact, with the problem of hermeneutics as well as with a certain number of others, and with some new perspectives which ought to be fruitful. This is the work of Wolfgang Pannenberg.

Pannenberg is not to be counted as one of the "hermeneutical theologians." Not that he, any more than the others, takes exception to or disdains the problem. In fact, he has made it the subject of an important article, "Hermeneutik und Universalgeschichte," in which he not only directly opposes the theses of Bultmann and his school, but analyzes and discusses in detail H. G. Gadamer's work on the philosophical problem of hermeneutics (*Wahrheit und Methods*). Nevertheless, Pannenberg feels that "it is not always necessary systematically to speak of hermeneutics in order to practice it" or in order to engage in fruitful reflections on the subject. His fundamental supposition is "that the hermeneutical problematic is suspended in principle within the concept of universal history, that it is, in other words, at once preserved as a moment and exceeded as a totality." For Pannenberg, the word of Scripture, like any other word, is absorbed in a wider reality which contains it and which it expresses. This reality is history. This history is the *thing* that the commentator seeks to interpolate into or append to the text which he must understand and interpret. But it is the same history which, in its continuity and its unity, allows the commentator really to cover the temporal distance separating him from the object of his investigation. It is history alone which can realize the "melting of horizons" of which Gadamer speaks, and which surely obscures the horizon of the commentator and the text to be interpreted. In fact, "only in the context of universal history can the *then* of the text be made to coincide with the *today* of the commentator in such a way that their temporal historical distance is not obliterated, but is at once bridged and preserved in the context of occurrence which unites them."

Without any doubt, the perspectives of universal history escape us in more than one respect, and from this point of view, Pannenberg never fails to keep aloof from Hegel and the Hegelianism of which he is so often accused. However, these perspectives have already been put forward "in the destiny of Jesus of Nazareth" insofar as in that destiny the consummation of all events has already been accomplished. For Pannenberg, the solution to the hermeneutical problem is to be found in the comprehension of this destiny and not in the comprehension of a simple word, or of any kerygma. We are once again returned to the Christological problem. We shall soon see that this problem will also be at the heart of the discussions which have revolved in the modern Catholic world about questions very much like those which disturb the Protestant world of our time.

CHAPTER FIVE

The Problem of Hermeneutics and Catholic Theology

CATHOLIC THEOLOGY has not ignored the problem of hermeneutics. Still, for Catholic theology—as for Protestant theology—it takes on a new aspect in our time, and it is this modern phase of the problem which we wish now to examine.

It can generally be said that the problem of hermeneutics appeared in Protestantism before it appeared in Catholicism. Apart from the bold efforts of a few, significantly Richard Simon, the method of radical criticism, initially almost destructive in its outlook, penetrated Protestant exegesis long before Catholic exegesis. The hermeneutical problem, though manifesting many similarities for Catholic and Protestant theology, nevertheless retains some aspects particular to each.

THE MODERNIST CRISIS

In practice, it was just at the moment of the modernist crisis that the renewed problem of hermeneutics became a problem of utmost urgency for Catholicism.

We shall not set forth the details of this laborious and often dramatic research which arose in Catholicism as a result of new methods of criticism in biblical exegesis. It will be enough to take a look at what seem to us the most important contributions. Even these contributions contain elements which are only of historical interest because, on the one hand, some of the problems raised by criticism have been replaced by others, and on the other, certain doctrinal conclusions have allowed certain reflections to evolve in a decisive way. However, most of the questions raised remain substantially our questions, and some of the insights gained in former controversies have never been improved upon. We would not be wasting our time in listening to those who, in our disrupted age, have literally spent their existence on the hermeneutical problem.

At this point, we must cite the work of M. J. Lagrange, an important representative of this basic research into the hermeneutical problem such as it presented itself in new terms to the Catholic consciousness at the turn of the century. In his *La Méthode historique*,[1] Lagrange summarized the conferences given at the Institut Catholique at Toulouse in 1902, adding an appendix entitled "Jesus and Criticism of the Gospels," which was a detailed critique of several theses held by Alfred Loisy in *L'Evangile et l'Eglise* (1902) and in *Autour d'un petit livre* (1903).[2]

In actual fact, only part of these conferences, which were addressed to a rather wide public, dealt directly with the subject at hand, the historical method. In other words, only part of them dealt with the problem of hermeneutics. In addition, the author announces in his Preface that his study concerns "above all, exegesis of the Old Testament." Later, he explains that his-

1. Paris, 1904.
2. Both published in Paris.

torical criticism is applied especially to the Old Testament because, by contrast with the New Testament, the Old covers a
sufficiently long period of time, and it is therefore possible to
recognize and follow a true development. This opinion is obviously typical of his time. Although the Old Testament spans
a longer period of time than the New, modern authors are
nevertheless solicitous of establishing for the latter not only a
chronology, but also a true development, a history. This concern is basic, for example, to Bultmann's *Theology of the New
Testament,* and it is acceptable also to Catholic exegetes. It will
be found in another form in a work such as Rudolf Schnackenburg's *God's Rule and Kingdom.*[3] Here we can also find a
development of the doctrine of eschatology within the New
Testament.

But for a criticism concerned primarily with the authenticity
of facts, the most pressing problems seemed to be those concerning the Old Testament. Above all, there was now less
interest in establishing and interpreting the origin and significance of the composition of the holy books than in directly
measuring their assertions against the established data of history,
and of science in general. That is why Lagrange is concerned
primarily with the problems of inspiration and inerrancy, and
to these alone he devotes an entire conference. In his works, as
in those of his contemporaries, apologetics seasoned with an
anti-Protestant polemic played a major role from beginning
to end.

Nevertheless, the major principles formulated by Lagrange
still dominate Catholic hermeneutics. This hermeneutics develops always between two poles which must never be confused,
nor may they be separated, and much less set against each other.
These two poles are faith and science, or, if we will, dogma

3. New York, 1964.

and history. As Lagrange explains in his Preface to the second edition, his entire work presupposes that the Bible is a composite matter. Also, his interpretation has two points of departure: "No Catholic exegete may presume to escape the dogmatic judgment of the Church, but neither may any authority protect our work, in its scientific aspects, from the judgment of competent men, nor yet prevent their verdict from being used against the Church, if our work is proved inadequate." If science, despite fluctuations in hypotheses, reveals much weakness, and risks making excessive claims, this danger is no less real for the constraint which has been made to arise from faith. "Alongside the dogmas of faith," Lagrange remarks, "which are the life of our souls, and the salvation of the world, and which neither the exegetes nor the Church, not even with a pious hand, may touch in order to change, there have sprung up a good number of so-called historical and literary dogmas. This was a light burden for the metaphysically oriented Middle Ages for which nothing was impossible to God. The same burden weighed already on the Renaissance, and Protestantism, eager to escape papal authority, happily took it up. But it became heavier and heavier with the more or less fortunate solutions of commentators, and absolutely unbearable for an age initiated into the knowledge of the ancient Orient. On this very point it is important to shed light and to listen to criticism. Still, infinite precaution is demanded here, for criticism must be prudent and circumspect; but it is good to know that we are entirely at liberty to profit from the knowledge of our time.

Because of the composite nature of this book wherein God's word is recorded, complementary duties follow for the exegete and the theologian. In specifying them, Lagrange gives answers beforehand to very specific problems which concern us even today. "Thus," he writes, "theologians who study contemporary dogma must never lose sight of the documents in which the dogma of the early Church is reflected, with all its genuine sincerity, and, for their part, exegetes have much to gain in never swerving from the authority of the Church. We pursue our manifold studies under the twin lights of revelation and reason, and reason does not contradict dogma, but neither is its search restricted by positive foregone conclusions, as long as it is not dealing with one of those very rare cases where the meaning of the text has been positively defined; and even in that case, criticism is able to follow its own methods. Under such conditions, obedience is not an irrational slavery, precisely because part of our study involves supernatural fact, of which we have not received a special revelation from God. But I maintain that we follow the right course in using the critical method without ever losing sight of the authority of the Church because it is the very maxim of the critical method to take environment into account, and the Church is precisely the environment of Scripture."

We will find ideas analogous to these in the writings of Maurice Blondel. His philosophical reflections will give them a strength and a depth as yet unsurpassed. This strength and this depth, moreover, were all the more indispensable because it was a question of reacting in the face of an exegetical enterprise of immense scope, undertaken with a superior talent, namely, the work of Alfred Loisy.

Clearly we cannot examine all of Loisy's theses, even if we confine ourselves to his booklet *L'Evangile et l'Eglise* which incited so much controversy, and particularly the criticism of Blondel. We will keep to the basic position he took in regard to the problem of hermeneutics, and refer especially to the explanations he himself gave of his work and his method in his very important correspondence with Blondel, which followed directly upon the publication of *L'Evangile et l'Eglise*.[4] More detailed information can be found, however, in the Preface to *L'Evangile et l'Eglise,* as well as in his *Autour d'un petit livre,* his *Etudes bibliques,* and his *Mémoires*.[5]

Loisy tried to be a strict and honest scholar. He outlined and developed his work on the historical level. To Abbé Wehrlé, who had misgivings about the Christology of the first two chapters of *L'Evangile et l'Eglise,* he replied, "You are infinitely better informed about my Christology than I am. The first two chapters contain only what is visible to the historian; thus, no Christology. My Christology is that of the Church, but I would add that I feel that this Christology admits of further explanation. . . . I am merely the humble decipherer of documents, and philosophy is not in my line" (*Au cœur de la crise moderniste,* p. 72).

He was aware, he claimed, of the limits of history. He wrote to Blondel that "There have been raised, and in reference to my book you yourself have raised problems which I had no intention of taking up or even of solving implicitly. Although the history therein may not be completely dissociated from other considerations [this was Blondel's objection] in the absolute meaning of your formula, it is nevertheless true that one can work on the factual level and thus arrive at conclusions which, though they may not reach the substance of things, still have an importance of their own. My book contains only one thesis: The Church is the Gospel continued; the development of Christianity is not something outside of or foreign to the Gospel. This can be proved by a serious study of history, if one disregards the divine character of the Gospel and the Church.

4. *Au coeur de la crise moderniste. Le dossier inédit d'une controverse,* Paris, 1960.
5. Paris, 1901; Paris, 1930–1931.

Since it cannot be proved all at once, such a *methodical* abstraction is most legitimate. The philosophy of history will therefore not be complete, but as the reader is warned of this, he does not have the right to quibble with the author" (*ibid.,* pp. 84–85).

We can see here that history, as the author conceives it, is more than a mere casual undertaking. What he has in mind is a complete apologetics of the Catholic religion: "It does not seem to me that many people have had the idea of a historical apologetics of religion," he wrote Blondel. "Well, this notion has been the passion of my existence" (*ibid.,* p. 82). He knew the effect of his method, of his exegesis, on theology itself: "I do not feel that my book implies the negation of any dogma. *It only implies the necessity of revising the entire teaching of theology from a historical perspective in order to render it more true, and from a philosophical perspective in order to make it theoretically more intelligible*" (*ibid.,* p. 85).

Loisy knew, he explained further, that Christian truth is not found solely in the historical data furnished by Scripture. "I did not say," he wrote Blondel, "that it would be necessary to return to the beginning of the development of Christianity in order to find the definitive and adequate expression of revealed truth. I had thought to refute Harnack, who claims it is necessary. But it is one thing to determine the historical personality of Christ, and another thing again to judge it from the point of view of faith. If it is a question of determining historical fact, then the Gospel can only be treated like any other historical source. And this is not to deny implicitly the supernatural in Christianity. You simply go so far as to suppress the Gospels as historical books, and do not see that, like the other theologians, you want me to find in the texts what is not there" (*ibid.,* p. 97). Loisy felt, moreover, that any expansion of Gospel data would be as detrimental to history as it would be to faith, which postulates history as well as respect for history's veracity. "What has come down to us in the Gospel," he wrote further, "reveals the tremendous influence of the work of Jesus, but we can only determine the initial and concrete form of this work through the documents which directly reflect the teaching and the activity of the Saviour. The apparent humility of this form can be to some extent a test of faith, but this would no more be a service to faith than it would be a negation of history. If you neglect or reject this historical form, you lose touch with reality, and unintentionally invite the historian to find that nothing substantial is known of the historical appearance of Jesus" (*ibid.,* p. 98).

* * *

It is easy to catch sight of, if not to discern, the precise demands as well as the ambiguities of the hermeneutical principles which Loisy calls his own. Maurice Blondel was immediately very much interested by the entire project, and at the same time moved by the agonizing questions which it necessarily posed. Loisy's work convinced him even more of the necessity for setting up what he called the "prolegomena to every future exegesis, . . . that is to say, a critical reflection on the very conditions of a science of revelation and of all sacred literature" (*op. cit.,* p. 90).

Before developing this critical reflection for its own sake, Blondel endeavored to understand what seemed disturbing to him, not only in this or that of Loisy's affirmations but also, and perhaps more basically, in the more or less covert presuppositions of his exegesis. While Loisy claimed to adhere to the range of fact and of history, he indeed proposed, as we have seen, a complete interpretation of Christianity. His history was, in principle, a theology. Blondel had reproached Loisy from the first for "disregarding the solidarity of the different sciences . . . and the interdependence of all human problems" (*ibid.,* p. 77) because he wanted to construct a pure history. But Loisy claimed that he was aware of this solidarity and that he, too, held that there could be no "dissociated history in the absolute sense" of Blondel's formula, and that the "historical knowledge of the Gospel would necessarily influence the concept of the supernatural in Christianity." Blondel expressed satisfaction with this, but in fact his misgivings were only increased. For did not this statement of Loisy's mean that history, that is, the concept of reality established by the scholar, will determine the nature of this reality by making everything conform to its niveau?

"I am delighted," replied Blondel, "to hear that you affirm this solidarity of questions on which I insist, so much so that I hope that scholarship and exegesis, in bringing us to terms with meaningful, simple, direct facts unencumbered by obstacles or cliches, will rejuvenate theology and piety. But here again I ask myself what will be the method, the law, the control of this renewal, for if history can in no way define the supernatural in Christianity, and you once indicated that it was in no way dependent on history, then it is not alone in conditioning its development; and it cannot by itself discern a legitimate and authentic connection with the forms which dogma assumes" (*op. cit.,* p. 101).

In these lines Blondel defined the aspect in which the problem of hermeneutics generally appears in Catholic theology today. As we shall later see, it is most often formulated as a pressing problem concerning the relation of exegesis and dogma. Blondel examined it progressively in his correspondence with Loisy, and proposed an analysis and authoritative solution of it under the title, *History and Dogma*.[6] The correspondence which we have already cited has allowed us to watch the movement and vicissitudes of his work as well as the impact that this firm and courageous intervention made on the Catholic world which was then in a state of confusion.

In this work, Blondel intended to remove in some way the conflict which had arisen between the proponents of the new historico-critical exegesis and those theologians who were satisfied to condemn them in the name of their formal principles. He felt that if the debate was to be settled effectively it would have to take place on a deeper level. "It is not enough," he said, "to determine by a preliminary examination the legitimate scope of the historical method and the rules of interpreting official documents. To do so would be to give them a different meaning because the rules of sacred hermeneutics and the necessary prolegomena to biblical criticism are themselves dominated by this at once old and new problem which we resolve" (*Les premiers écrits,* p. 151).

Blondel then proceeded to show the shortcomings of the solutions which have been given to date regarding the relation between faith and history which is implied in any application of "sacred hermeneutics." According to him, *"extrinsicism* and *historicism* are, in regard to the essential problem which faces the Christian conscience today, two diversely incomplete solutions, and equally dangerous for the faith. While these are two extreme and opposed viewpoints, they are similar in kind and based on the same spiritual attitude, and they suffer from analogous philosophical lacunae, aggravating each other by their very conflict" (*ibid.,* p. 154).

With regard to extrinsicism, history is only the starting point of a system in which the real content and the concrete meaning

6. In *Les premiers écrits de Maurice Blondel,* Paris, 1956.

of the data are not related. The abstractly "miraculous" or "supernatural" character of the facts would in some way sanction the construction of a complete system, which would only be dependent on itself. The important thing would be to establish *that* God has acted and spoken and not to examine *what* he said and did by human instruments" (*ibid.,* p. 158). We easily see the treachery of this position with regard to the object of faith. But this haughty and irritating attitude also reveals great weakness when confronted by the renewed attacks of historical exegesis.

Faced with extrinsicism, historicism (which arises in part from it) also presents some equally great shortcomings and equally serious lacunae. Under the appearance of being scrupulously faithful to reality, it imposes a domination as tyrannical as dogmatic extrinsicism, for it tries to reduce reality to its own predetermined concepts, and make it abide by its laws. It forgets the solidarity of the different levels of knowledge, which corresponds to the solidarity of the elements of reality. Under the pretext of a necessary abstraction from method, while imperceptibly making this method absolute, it imposes a naturalist or positivist, or we might say, abstract outlook on historical reality. The illusion and the perversity of historicism is this alternating substitution of history-reality for history-science by a sort of infinitesimal oscillation which continually renews the ambiguity of its simultaneously true and false pronouncements, compelling the reader to squint painfully" (*ibid.,* p. 170).

For Blondel, critical exegesis must remain open exegesis, at once aware of what it is involved with, and aware that it cannot itself perceive reality, which always surpasses its image as found in a document. What is true to some degree of all reality, is true to a greater extent of that deeply mysterious reality of untold depth, which is Jesus Christ. We say this not only because

we believe in his divine character, but also because what the
texts tell us about Jesus can only be "the consciousness of his
consciousness," or, we might say, of his intimacy, enjoyed by
limited men of equally limited means. Even before faith in-
tervenes to confess with certainty and precision who Jesus Christ
is, simple reflection would force us to admit that there the real
Christ is more the one met by critical history, and that therefore critical history, even on the level of historical reality, must
remain aware of its limits and its basic incompetence to make
any absolute pronouncements. "The foundations of Christianity,"
Blondel tells us, "cannot be thought of as being established
solely on some testimonies and texts, on simple literary records,
or on a portrait. There can be, and there must be another
thread linking us with Christ, another history made of living
relics, without which Christianity would be no more than a
religion of parchments and scribes, —without which it would
not exist" (ibid., p. 181).

Thus dogma, which expresses the faith of this Church which
itself proceeds from the total action of Christ, so far from
limiting the work of history from without by imposing on it
alien standards, is able, on the contrary, to clarify it from
within, just as history, on its own level, can contribute to a
better understanding of dogmatic definitions. The common fault
of extrinsicism and historicism is that both disregard the true
nature of tradition. It is in the living reality of tradition that
history and dogma, critical exigency and the demands of faith,
find their respective meaning and concur to let us meet the
phenomenal reality which is Christianity, which is their ultimate
common goal. It is only in tradition that the interpretation of
biblical texts does not a priori pervert its outline, and proves
itself faithful to its total objective.

History and dogma, or if we prefer, critical exegesis and

dogmatic theology, are still the two poles between which the work of fathoming the realities of faith takes place in the Catholic Church. As we have said, it is in the search for a dialogue, difficult but necessary, between exegetes and dogmatists, that we will find what seems to us to correspond best, in Catholic theology, to the research on the hermeneutical problem within Protestant theology.

Before we view this dialogue we must pause for a while to study the confessional difficulties relevant to the way in which the problem of hermeneutics is posed and the solution which is sought.[7]

HERMENEUTICS AND TRADITION

In defending historicism, Blondel initiates us into a fundamental criticism of one type of Protestant hermeneutics.

We have seen the tension and opposition engendered in Protestant theology over the problem of hermeneutics. The urgency and gravity assumed by the problem of hermeneutics in Protestant theology is due to the relation, introduced by the Reformation, between Scripture and tradition, and more generally, between Scripture and the Church. We do not wish to imply that it is only because of the principle of *sola Scriptura* that Protestantism has rejected tradition as an aid to the understanding of Scripture which represents the traditional faith of the Church and that, therefore, its presentation of the problem of the adequate examination of the Bible should have been

7. The period between the modernist crisis and our own age has been omitted deliberately. Our intention was not to give a detailed history of the hermeneutical problem but rather to reflect on the most important moments of its history, and these are certainly its beginnings after the turn of the century, and its development today.

considerably more urgent and hazardous than it was. But, as Ebeling has rightly pointed out, the Reformation introduced a new hermeneutical principle, and this principle, which modern theologians characterize as radically "historical," does not seem far different from what Blondel calls historicism.

For Blondel, what characterized historicism, its limits, and its basic faults was its abstraction in relation to a historical reality which is never identified with the representations, the "images" of the text. Now, before being expressed in an "abstract" relation to the text, this "abstraction" was historically expressed in a breach, an alienation in regard to secular tradition, which was viewed with some suspicion. The basic characteristic of the Reformation was its concern to recover a *direct* relation to the texts of Scripture.

At certain times in their history Catholics have undoubtedly lived too far removed from sacred Scripture, which should continually have been a source of strength for their faith, since it remains for them the primary instrument of God's word as well as a rule of faith. But they never thought that the substance of revelation was transmitted by the scriptural text alone and that a direct rapport with the text was the only authentic rapport, or even that it was to be promoted at all costs. The encounter of a Catholic with Jesus Christ, and his initiation into the faith, is not usually the result of merely reading the Bible. Rather, this takes place through baptism and integration into the life of the Church which, by its teaching, by its liturgy, by the witness of its saints continues to reveal the riches of the "manifold grace" of God, and to evoke a more and more personal and total adherence to salvific realities. The Church does not understand itself merely as the community of those who correctly understand, in faith, God's word contained in Scripture, but also as the locus and the guardian, established by the Lord, of a *tradition* in which his thought is authentically preserved and in which, consequently, the very substance of Scripture continually bears the fruits of salvation.

If the particular problem of hermeneutics taken up by Bultmann is in the form of the challenging and dramatic problem of demythologization, is it not because it is raised by a theologian who wants to encounter without any intermediary the word of faith of men who are separated from him by two thousand years? Hence inevitably the vertiginous feeling that there is a real chasm to be bridged. It seems that Bultmann once more expresses in his ultimate conclusions what could be called the Protestant adventure.

Thus, the hermeneutical problem could not assume in Catholicism the same urgency and the same character it has in Protestantism. Nevertheless, the problem could be entirely ignored only if the Catholic world were rather indifferent in regard to the scriptural sources of its faith.

In his long introduction to Louis Bouyer's *The Spirit and Forms of Protestantism*,[8] Guy de Broglie on the contrary, has no difficulty in alluding to the primacy of the Scripture argument in Catholic theology. Even if Scripture is not the unique locus where the Church rediscovers the revelation of her Lord, this locus still, in certain respects, contains it completely. For the Church, Scripture is preëminently the "canon" of faith. And it is a fact that the magisterium has never thought to define any dogma without showing that it is in some way contained in Scripture. The Catholic Church has continually drawn directly from the scriptural sources of its faith in order to nourish it and safeguard its purity. If not in all its members (for it would have been difficult before the invention of the printing press

8. Westminster, 1956.

and the spread of culture), the Church has continued to do so in the person of pastors and theologians.

Throughout the centuries, Catholic theologians have generally studied the problem of hermeneutics in relation to the *sense* or *senses* of the Scriptures they meditated, rather than as one of the more or less subjective requisites of correct interpretation.

The opposition between the problem of hermeneutics such as it is envisaged by modern Protestant theologians and the traditional problem of the senses of Scripture should not be overestimated. The modern problem of hermeneutics in some respects indeed consists in trying to find the meaning of Scripture while asking how the text ought to be approached so that the truth of this meaning is revealed to the reader or the exegete. This problem of the sense or senses of Scripture necessarily implies determining the angle or perspective from which the text was envisaged when it shows this or that sense. Moreover, this is why the theology in question speaks of different senses, literal, moral, spiritual, and so forth. Finally, in the hermeneutical preoccupation of modern Protestantism, the accent is on the *a priori* conditions necessary for a faithful reading of Scripture, and this dominates the concern for correctness. In the quest for the sense or senses of Scripture, the accent, on the contrary, is on the fullness of content which faith presupposes in Scripture, by which faith knows itself to have been nourished even before it begins its investigation.

Thus, one should not try to see too categorical an opposition between the problem of hermeneutics found in the preoccupations of many contemporary Protestant theologians and the traditional problem of the sense of Scripture which can be followed in the older Catholic tradition. It would be an oversimplification to state that the problem of biblical hermeneutics as such can concern only Protestant theology, and that the problem of the sense or senses of Scripture is the monopoly of Catholic theology. We have already looked briefly at the essence of the Catholic problem of hermeneutics, and we shall now try to be more explicit. If it is true that Luther at times showed a certain contempt for medieval or patristic speculation on the senses of Scripture, then the attitude of the Reformers in regard to the Bible, such as a Karl Barth recommends, was not greatly different from what we find today with a good many Protestant theologians of hermeneutics. Most of the Reformers were scarcely preoccupied with the subjective conditions of a valid approach to and a valid examination of the Scriptures, and so the import of scriptural witness seemed to them based on pure evidence. According to Luther, Scripture is *"per sese certissima, facillima, apertissima, sui ipsius interpres, omnius omnia probans, judicans et illuminans."*

Actually, this absolute objectivism, which brings to nought the subjective conditions of appropriation, ought not to be thought of as merely the opposite of anxious research which tends to exhaust itself in determining these subjective conditions. The absolute objectivism of the Reformers and the transcendental reflections of modern theologians on hermeneutics stem from the same neglect of the mediation of history, or if we prefer, from the same neglect of living tradition as the fundamental instrument of revelation. For Catholicism, the meaning of this revelation contained in Scripture is neither a purely objective *datum* imposed on the understanding considered as the faculty of evidence, nor the fruit of an adjustment always better controlled by our questioning. This meaning informs the tradition of the Church, which alone is its entire manifestation.

It will be objected that the Reformers did not ignore the subjective conditions of an appropriation in faith of the meaning of Scripture. According to them, in fact, along with evidence which reveals the meaning of Scripture, the interior witness of the Holy Spirit must be added. Inversely, the Bultmannian theologians of hermeneutics always presuppose the *encounter* of this living word witnessed by the scriptural text, an encounter that cannot be effectively brought about by exegetical questioning. However, in both cases especially, scriptural truth and appropriation in faith tend to be considered from the outset as having an autonomous existence and being in danger of remaining apart from one another. The Catholic Church lives on the conviction that the gift of the Holy Spirit does not consist in an independent light thrown on the historical manifestation of the meaning of Scripture, and that this historical manifestion is merged with the Church itself. Thus, the discovery of this meaning can no more be made apart from the totality of this history in which it is realized, than it can be made apart from the hierarchical institution which assures its authenticity. The Church discovers and possesses the unchangeable meaning of the divine discourse contained in Scripture by extending it. It is this meaning which determines its origin as its only complete manifestation.

It remains to specify *how* the meaning of Scripture is brought to light in the Church. To say that discovery of the meaning of Scripture is not effected independently of the totality of history wherein it is realized, nor of the hierarchical institution which assures its authenticity, does not necessarily mean that this discovery is made automatically or exclusively *by* just any sudden movement of history or *by* the authoritarian directives of the hierarchy. To depart from an idealism more or less tainted with mysticism or intellectualism is not necessarily the same as professing some kind of religious positivism or pragmatism for which the meaning of Scripture would be immediately given or recognizable in some historical figure, determined and assimilated to the very reality of the Church, which is the direct and adequate expression of God's thought on the world. Catholicism has not been spared this criticism of being tainted with "ecclesiastical positivism." More than once it has been declared that the Church considers as the very standard of what ought to be, only those things which develop within its confines. Likewise it has been maintained that as far as the Church is concerned, pastoral or even utilitarian considerations, those which concern its cohesion and stability, outweigh the very concern for truth. In such perspectives, the problem of hermeneutics could obviously have no place. The word of revelation should be given and would have to be received in the manner of a deposit.

Aside from the veneration with which the Catholic Church has continually surrounded the very text of Scripture, its doctrine of inspiration obviously does not allow any such judgment. It is true that the New Testament is essentially that new covenant, founded on the blood of Christ, whose fulfillment is the Church. But for the Church itself the New Testament is a kind of charter recording its foundation, and in which it rediscovers its own meaning. The preservation of the text contributes in a preëminent and indispensable way to making the progress of the Church's life as it continues through the ages— in somewhat linear fashion—continually return to its origins— in somewhat circular fashion. From these origins is its strength made manifest, and in them the Church always finds its legitimacy and authenticity.

We must admit that this "meditation" of the Church on its origin recalled in all its purity by the text of Scripture, amounts to a direct rapport, but only in one aspect. For the Church does this by disregarding her memory, which contains at once the original word and the meaning which precisely this word has developed in the course of centuries and which must remain unchanged. Thus, the Church can never entertain the concept of bridging a gap, a concept which can result in part from an illusion which Bultmann tells us is experienced in meditating on the texts of Scripture.

Does the memory of the Church prevent Catholic theology from encountering original documents in their true significance? Is it capable of remaining open to the revelations of science, history, and criticism? Undoubtedly the Catholic Church is convinced of the possibility of a fundamental accord between faith on the one hand, and on the other, the truths given by science, which it is resolutely determined to respect. Nevertheless a certain tension is liable to appear in practice between the affirmations of the one and the phenomena which the others try to define. The modernist crisis of which we have spoken specifically represents one of the most dramatic examples of this tension, and was occasioned among other things by the extraordinary development of the various scientific and critical disciplines.

Less tragically, a tension is often manifested today between the representatives of complementary disciplines, or, more simply, between exegetes and theologians. That age has passed when one and the same man—such as Origen—could be at once exegete, theologian, and spiritual master. As it developed, criticism became more and more demanding and called for a specialization stimulated more and more by those who were dedicated to it. The integration which at another time could have been wrought at the level of one individual, can now be made only at the level of the ecclesiastical body. In the Catholic Church the work of the exegete is only one *instance,* if an essential one, of the effort to understand the message of faith which is certainly already contained in substance in Scripture, but which, as we have said, developed its meaning throughout the life of the Church and in all its forms.

EXEGESIS AND DOGMATICS

As we have seen, exegetes and dogmatic theologians see more and more clearly the necessity for a dialogue which is both firm and comprehensive. This dialogue, which fortunately has begun, defines a preoccupation and a research best corresponding in the Catholic world to the reflections and discussions on the problem of hermeneutics in the Protestant world.

Under the title *Exegese und Dogmatik,*[9] a number of interesting contributions to the problem of hermeneutics—which is far from being solved—have been collated. This book certainly gives evidence of a crisis: if there had not been any difficulty, if accord between the research of the exegete and the teaching of the theologian had been immediately realized, there would be no need to point out its necessity or to analyze its conditions. But it gives evidence also of the active preoccupation of making two points of view supplement each other and better agree without losing their distinctiveness. Of the nine studies in this work, four are directly related to this very problem of the relations of exegesis to dogmatics. Two of the studies are the works of the dogmatic theologians Karl Rahner and Edward Schillebeeckx, and two the works of the exegetes Anton Vögtle and Rudolf Schnackenburg.

The contribution of Rahner, *Exegese und Dogmatik,* is the most important and vigorous. Rahner reproaches the exegetes for too often forgetting or seeming to forget that they are

9. Herbert Vorgrimler, ed., Mayence, 1962. Translated as *Dogmatic versus Biblical Theology,* Baltimore and London, 1966.

Catholic theologians. Catholic exegesis is not, in fact, a philology or a part of the history of religions. Rather is it a "division of Catholic theology," and is "interior" to it. The faith of the Church is not merely a *norma negativa* for exegesis, but a *positive principle of research,* whatever might be the scientific rigor with which this research should be undertaken.

The Catholic exegete should not be content with raising problems, still less with giving in to the temptation of embarrassing his fellow theologians, or of taking malicious pleasure in their failures (*Schadenfreude*). He should usually be able to show that his exegesis agrees, not only negatively, but even positively with the traditional doctrine of the Church, and if he does not reach his goal he ought at least to remember that this is his own failure.

Rahner deplores the fact that the exegetes do not always approach the matter seriously enough. They lay claim to a theology which would better be grounded in Scripture. But, at the same time, they often look jealously upon their colleagues in dogmatic theology who meddle in exegesis but have no license in that profession. And the exegetes themselves give way under the problems raised by exegesis.

Furthermore, if exegetes knew their theology better, if they applied themselves to it with more conviction and put more effort into it, they would not find such simplistic opposition as they believe themselves obliged to raise between theology and the findings of their own critical research. It is necessary to start with a quite *primitive* doctrine of the Trinity in order to maintain that such a doctrine is not found in St. Paul, and that the Apostle purely and simply identifies the *Kyrios* and the *Pneuma* (an allusion to a book dedicated to this theme: *Kyrios und Pneuma,* 1961). Exegetes ought to concern themselves with showing—and this is an essential aspect of their work—that

differences of language can be reconciled with the affirmation
of a truth which is substantially the same.

Finally, knowing enough to distinguish between the different
levels of readers or hearers to whom, of their very nature, their
works are addressed, the exegetes ought to consider those who
are weak in the faith and those who require much explanation
before they understand. They should take care to point out to
the other members of the Church that the purpose of their
work, despite its critical aspects, is not to destroy but to build.

The exegetes, however, are not alone responsible for the
crisis which today affects the relation between exegesis and
dogmatics. Dogmatic theologians also play a part in this crisis
which Rahner tried to analyze.

If exegetes too often appear unconcerned with holding to the
tradition of the Church and with fostering theological reflection,
dogmatic theologians for their part generally take little notice
of the considerable amount of work accomplished in our day by
exegesis. The dogmatic theologian ought to put himself in the
best possible situation for correctly understanding the word of
God. It is thus his obligation to be concerned with exegesis, and
with exegesis "*as it is to be practised today,* not as it was in the
good old days" (p. 36). He must also understand and respect
the point of view of the exegete and the historian, which is not
and should not be his. Therefore, when he sees conclusions
formulated which do not directly correspond to his own, he
should not be eager to condemn them by citing Denzinger, or
a phrase from an encyclical, in order peremptorily to declare
that "this is not so."

This respect for the work of the exegete and for his difficulties, this good will in face of his audacity, this patience
with his apparent lack of prudence are not demanded of the
dogmatic theologian solely on the basis of charity and of the

understanding required towards a discipline different from his own. They are also required by the Catholic understanding of the faith. This understanding has always challenged fideism, and has reserved to fundamental theology its proper place which, while being entirely directed towards faith, should not merely use it as its starting point. It is the duty of the exegete to work as a true historian with the resources proper to him, and above all with critical reason.

Moreover, the exegete will not discover immediately, nor such as they are, the dogmas elaborated by the Church in the course of the centuries. The exegete "not only can but must express himself with more nuances than the dogmatic theologians," and this is usually to the advantage of all concerned. His obligation is to present the texts as they are, perhaps with the ambiguities they may retain, as well as with the riches which have not been exploited within the scope of dogmatic theology.

Taking into account the various possible ways of approaching the reality of faith, and examining his own thought, the dogmatic theologian can and must abundantly contribute towards clarifying the work of the exegete. He would free him by showing that the results his criticism affords are far less irreconcilable with the true demands of traditional faith than it might appear. Thus he could, or rather he must, specify the *sui generis* character of the appearances of Jesus after the resurrection, which do not signify a pure and simple return to the world of common experience. Thus, too, he can better show the strict connection between the aspects of "theology" and "economy" in trinitarian or christological doctrine, so that the New Testament data on this subject would more easily appear at bottom the same as that of traditional theology. Similarly, a Christology which would not be constructed merely in terms of the concept of the "assumption" of human nature by the Word, but which would start from the consideration of Christ as Son of Mary and head of humanity would render a more faithful account of the Gospel data on the "growth" of Jesus in age and in wisdom, on the "ignorance" of the Son about the day of judgment. In this regard, a more profound study of the meaning of the verb "to know," which is not equivocal, as well as of the very broad concept of the "historical," would likewise be of immense value. Dogmatic theologians should also examine their own categories and not sit in judgment on a perfect science, not even listening to those who come under their judgment.

In the reflections which conclude this very candid confrontation of exegete and dogmatic theologian, Rahner emphasizes above all the importance of the climate of confidence which should pervade the Catholic Church so that questions can develop. If a word of warning, or a condemnation, may be necessary from time to time in order to close off a path which is manifestly and gravely false, only this development of questions in frank discussion, in the sincere confrontation of points of view, is capable of directing thought to that truth which enlightens us and makes us free.

Edward Schillebeeckx develops some analogous ideas on a more theoretical level in his *Exegese, Dogmatik und Dogmenentwicklung*.[10] In particular, he analyzes, in some thoughts akin to those of Blondel, the relation of exegesis and dogmatics in terms of the idea of development. In a way, he suggests a dynamics of theological endeavor.

He shows once more that exegesis and dogmatics have each their own fields of endeavor. The first must concern itself pri-

10. See also his *Christ the Sacrament of the Encounter with God*, New York, 1963.

marily with establishing what the authors and contemporaries of Scripture grasped, what they understood of the word of God, and the second must show "how this same word, heard in the past by Israel and by the apostolic Church and still addressed also to us men of the twentieth century, is to be understood by us without being diverted from its meaning" (p. 99). The exegete should have no "desire to find in holy Scripture later dogmas *as such*" (p. 98). And it would be false method to want to put them there. If, however, despite the divergent perspective and the actual difference of their propositions, exegesis and dogmatics can and must agree in the substance of their teaching, it is because there is an "internal dynamics" in Scripture which surpasses everything that purely philosophical and literary methods can establish, because the realities which Scripture contains and of which it is a witness are, according to an expression of G. Auzou, "realities in action,"[11] or again, it is because there is a *sensus plenior* which, although initially given, is revealed only progressively in the course of history.

To discover this *sensus plenior* in all its fullness, but also in its authenticity, the exegete and the dogmatic theologian both have a role, and these roles are at once different and complementary. In the progress that constitutes the reflection of the Church on its faith, "dogmatics fulfills a role and a service which it cannot and must not leave exclusively to Christian exegesis and biblical theology. On the other hand, exegesis fulfills a critical function in relation to dogmatics, for the exegete studies the origin sanctioned by God and the impulse which he gives, an impulse which because of its original orientation will remain a critical moment always superior to its own sequence" (pp. 113–114).

While the exegete insists on the demands made by his own

11. See George Auzou, *The Word of God,* St. Louis, 1960.

field and the formidable problems it poses, he appears capable of understanding such a language of his colleagues in dogmatic theology.

"It is precisely because he is a Catholic exegete," Anton Vögtle remarks, "that the specialist on the New Testament— for everyone recognizes that today the most serious problems arise in regard to the New Testament—must examine the texts in a thoroughly concrete way." This means that he must examine them without making them say anything other than what they do say (p. 55). Does not the New Testament speak to us with invincible authority of the most essential realities of the faith: the salvific event accomplished in Jesus Christ, the relation of Christ to the Father and to the Spirit, the Church. . . ? Must we not therefore always seek correctly to understand the New Testament in its new context?

However, the New Testament does not and cannot directly reply to all our questions, nor to all those which the Church has posed in the course of her history, particularly when it has penetrated other cultures and put to work different modes of thought. Furthermore, the information that the exegete supplies, while remaining faithful to its object, will always run the risk of appearing "deficient," if not contrary to what has been established by later theology, so that there will be at times a suspicion of a lack of Catholic understanding. It is, rather, the duty of the exegete to protect the text from "calculating" or tendentious interpretation (p. 61). Hasty, overly facile agreement usually results in a loss of the fullness contained, perhaps vaguely but still really, in the deposit of revelation. Such precipitate statements can be found even within the New Testament (see the usage made by Matthew and Luke of the Marcan source): we read in Mark 3, 21, for example, that the brethren of Jesus wished to restrain him because he was "beside himself." This detail seemed inadmissible to the other two evangelists. So it is true that we are inclined to judge the data of a text by our ideas, rather than our ideas by these data, as soon as they take us by surprise.

"It is normal," Vögtle continues, that new ideas astonish, even overwhelm at first, those who meet them unprepared, independent of the long and painstaking work of preparation by which these new ideas are revealed, and in which, moreover, they often assume a different meaning than for those who approach them only superficially. Has not the layman been easily shocked more than once by certain dogmatic statements which do not exactly correspond to what he has learned from the catechism or the theological manuals? In both cases, let us know enough to trust in those who, animated by the spirit of the Church, loyally pursue the truth. The exegesis and theology of the New Testament have, and know that they have, an irreplaceable function because of the very object of their efforts. But they are nonetheless convinced of their own role of servants, *ancillae* to the theological enterprise as a whole. Far from being inflated by their progress, they have rather become more aware of their limitations. "As never before, the search of the past few decades has made the New Testament specialist aware that the New Testament is not an independent reality in itself, which was established before the Church or apart from it or as a self-sufficient authority, responsible only to itself in relation to a Church called into existence by the Pentecost" (p. 68). More than ever, perhaps, the New Testament specialist knows that the object of his study is inconceivable apart from that Church which is the authentic interpreter of "its own holy Scripture" (*ibid.*).

In his *Zur dogmatischen Auswertung des Neuen Testaments,* Rudolf Schnackenburg also emphasizes the useful critical function of exegesis in regard to dogmatics. Exegesis must restrain superficial speculation, or at least make clear, on occasion, the frailty of the foundations to which it bears witness. Thus it will prevent us from drawing too many conclusions about the nature of the glorified bodies from the fact that Luke represents the risen Lord as eating with his disciples. It will adduce other texts which will show the true meaning of this detail given by the evangelist (such as Mk. 12, 25: "they are as the angels in heaven"). Many another example of such valuable correctives, asserts Schnackenburg, may be adduced, for example the number of the elect, the virgin birth, and so forth (see pp. 125–127).

A serious exegesis, however, can resolve the problems presented by certain texts better than could certain alien distinctions from speculative theology, for example, "the Father is greater than I" (Jn. 14, 28): the answer of St. John Chrysostom or of St. Augustine to the effect that this verse treats only of the human nature of Christ is certainly far less adequate than those found in the perspectives of the history of salvation, which are those of the New Testament (pp. 122–123).

Finally, exegesis can be of great service to the dogmatic theologian in his very positive task of translating the content of faith into a language which speaks to the man of today. For there is more than one analogy between certain essential modes of modern thought and the mode of "historical and dynamic thought of the Bible" (p. 123).

In any case, far from being at cross purposes, the work of the exegete and the dogmatic theologian, if performed in the spirit of dialogue, not only must supplement each other, but also must be of mutual service in the most fruitful and constructive way.

* * *

Is not Catholicism the locus par excellence of this dialogue? Surely it is for this reason also the locus in which the word of God can always be understood in its veracity.

In the same way as this "immediate" relation which we have mentioned as characteristic of the Protestant preoccupation, the relation of the exegete to the word of God, because it represents a single point of view is, of itself, an "abstract" relation. And the relation of the dogmatic theologian to the living word is always menaced by the same abstraction which leads to the "extrinsicism" which Blondel analyzed, and which makes much too little of the concrete, historical, inexhaustible data of revelation.

Nevertheless, if they are to be true to their vocations, Catholic exegetes and dogmatic theolgians both must concentrate on the concrete reality of the word of God which they have to translate and which lives in the Church. The witness of this reference is the relationship of mutual understanding in the communion of the same faith, certified by submission to the same magisterium. The tensions which remain in this fundamental understanding, its incompleteness, show that the believer is always *in via,* that he never *is* the Church, and that the Church, while the reality of revelation can truly be found in it, nevertheless continually needs to seek it out and be reformed by it.

Postface

IN THE COURSE of this investigation we have deliberately confined ourselves to formal questions, to the hermeneutical problem *per se*. Had we attempted to combine questions of content with questions of form, and to devote attention not only to the problem of examining Scripture and tradition but also to their actual meaning, we would have had to involve a whole new field of research and, in fact, to write another book. On the other hand, we have tried to show that what constitutes the novelty of current research on the hermeneutical problem is the reflection—in more or less wide perspectives—on the *a priori* conditions for true interpretation of Scripture and, in general, of every object of interest for our existence and our faith. We have emphasized at times the pitfalls and the constrictions that such perspectives may easily involve. Still, they answer to needs which it is impossible to ignore.

In concluding, we would like to call attention to the research on the meaning of Scripture recorded not only in works of purely scientific analysis, but also in contemporary works of authentic biblical theology.

Rudolf Bultmann, for example, has offered a rich interpretation of passages and whole books of the New Testament, summarized in his masterly *Theology of the New Testament*.[1]

Gerhard von Rad has circumscribed his *Old Testament The-*

1. New York, 1951 (vol. I) and 1955 (vol. II).

ology[2] with a number of brief but profound hermeneutical reflections. A collection of these essays has recently appeared under the title *Probleme alttestamentlicher Hermeneutik.*[3]

Important among the relevant works of Catholic authors are the following: *Themes of the Bible*[4] by Jacques Guillet, *The Meaning of Sacred Scripture*[5] by Louis Bouyer, *The Christian Approach to the Bible*[6] by Celestin Charlier, and especially *Sens chrétien de l'Ancien Testament*[7] by Pierre Grelot.

Let us now hope for a more intensive and far-reaching study of the hermeneutical problem, which would surely bring to light new points of contact and a meaningful continuity between our time and all foregoing Christian history.

2. New York, 1962 (vol. I) and 1966 (vol. II).
3. Munich, 1960.
4. Notre Dame, 1960.
5. Notre Dame, 1958.
6. Westminster, 1962.
7. Paris and Tournai, 1962. See especially pp. 408f.

Index of Names